DATE DUE

DEMCO 38-296

Copyright 1983

TABLE OF CONTENTS

	Page
Chapter I Geology	1
Chapter II Early Indians	19
Chapter III Explorers (1673-1780)	38
Chapter IV Trailblazers (1780-1805)	49
Chapter V Time of Conflict (1805-1832)	61
Chapter VI Settling (1832-1838)	78
Chapter VII Path to Statehood (1838-1846)	94
Chapter VIII Bound for Iowa (1845-1865)	110
Chapter IX Building the Cornbelt (1865-1890)	140
Chapter X Protest and Reform (1890-1920)	166
Chapter XI Moving to Town (1920-1950)	193
Index	215

CHAPTER I
Introduction

Geologic time is not clocked by equal intervals such as years, centuries or even thousands of years. Geologic time is measured by events of importance such as successions of volcanic eruptions, land being drowned by seas, mountains being thrust upward, evolution and extinction of prehistoric animals and expansion and melting of glaciers. Any one of these events may take millions of years. Most of us can't comprehend the enormous amounts of time involved in even the most simple geologic function. The earth has been developing for about 4.5 billion years if we believe in radioisotope dating of meteorite fragments and moon rock samples. The basement or the crystalline

rocks beneath Iowa were formed from molten materials that were liquid because of intense heat. They cooled and hardened into rocks called igneous (ig-ne-us) rocks about 1.4 billion years ago. Later, the shell of the earth bulged and cracked. Earthquakes caused the rock crust to buckle and change in shape.

After these igneous rocks were formed and rearranged, shallow seas covered the state from 600 to 80 million years ago. These seas formed layers of sedimentary rock, or rock composed of small grains of minerals and small marine organisms. Then during the last 2.0 (two) million years until about 13,000 years ago, glaciers of the Ice Age came and melted away over Iowa. They left behind most of the material from which modern soil developed. Thus in terms of geologic time, most of Iowa's landscape features and the materials from which they are made are very "young".

To look at the age of Iowa's land, geologists use the carbon-14 or radiocarbon method to date events within the last 40,000 years. This method measures the amount of radioactive carbon remaining in fossil plants and animals. Over the years, a once-living organism loses amounts of radioactive material at a known set rate.

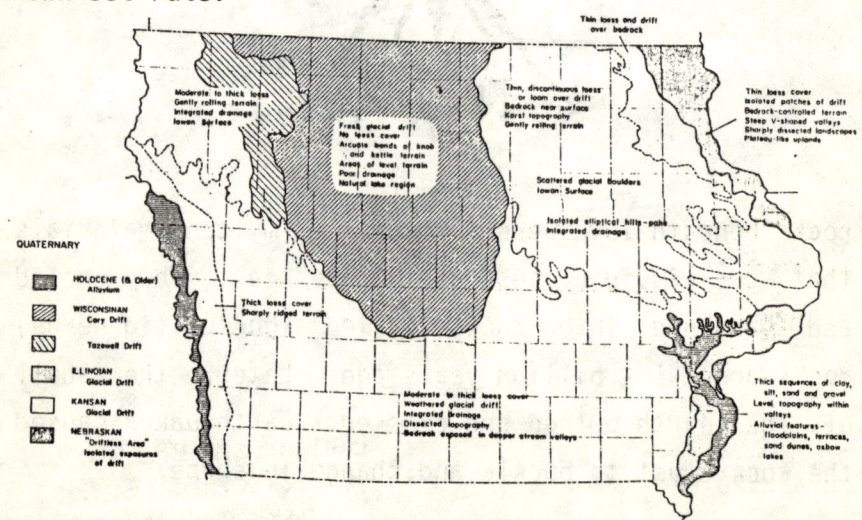

Iowa's land is characterized by low elevations, relatively gentle slopes and many rivers and streams. Although glaciers are responsible for Iowa's level terrain, it will be seen later on that these glaciers also made Iowa different.

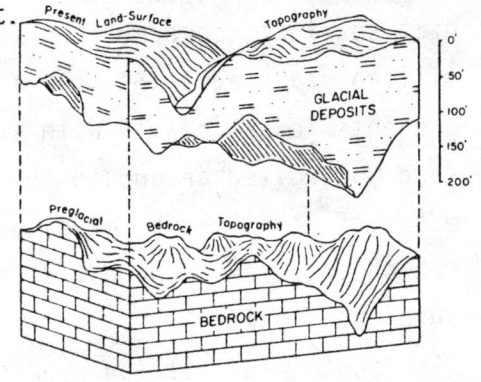

The Rock Record

To understand the development of Iowa's present landscape, it must first be understood that Iowa has a buried landscape composed of materials laid down in the ancient environments mentioned earlier. Each change in environment made a different type of rock. As was mentioned, the earliest rocks, now well below our present surface, were formed from heated molten rock that cooled and hardened. Examples of these igneous rocks are granite, basalt and gabbro. At this time, Iowa was part of a large mountain range. Over millions of years, many of these mountains were leveled by erosion.

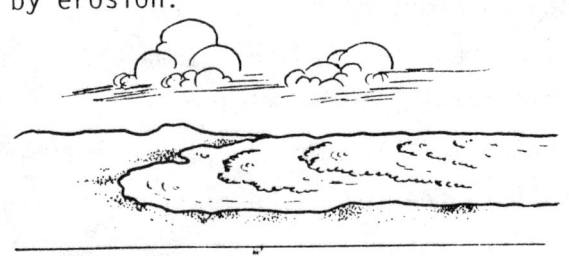

3

The next era of rock formation resulted in sedimentary rocks composed chiefly of quartz. Quartz is composed of silica (the main element in sand). The sand in Iowa's <u>sandstones</u> was deposited near the edge of a sea that covered the United States over 500 million years ago. At that time, Iowa looked like the present Texas coast with vast beaches of sand. The sand was rolled around in the shallow water at the edge of the sea by waves and currents. Eventually, the grains were rounded and compressed under pressure into sandstone.

About 475 million years ago, the seas deposited layers of lime which hardened into limestone as the sea retreated. Iowa now looked like a low coastal plain and was exposed to weathering and erosion.

INVERTEBRATES

The seas returned about 450 million years ago and deposited another layer of sandstone, rocks and additional layers of limestone. These rocks are crammed with fossils of invertebrate sea animals. They also contain the minerals lead and zinc that were later deposited along cracks in the rocks. These deposits are responsible for Iowa becoming one of America's important lead mining districts in the 1800s. Late in this period, vast quantities of mud were washed into the sea. These muddy layers formed shale.

MILLIONS OF YEARS AGO	ROCK LAYERS
500	QUARTZ, GRANITE, BASALT
475	LIMESTONE
450	SANDSTONE LEAD ZINC SHALE
440	MORE LIMESTONE
425	CLAY, SHALE
310	MORE SANDSTONE LIMESTONE SHALE CLAY SILTSTONE COAL
265	NO ROCK LAYER LAID DOWN - BUT THE EVAPORATION OF SEA WATER FORMED GYPSUM

Keep in mind these impressive changes and rock-forming histories did not occur in a lifetime. Thousands of human generations could live and die in the time that one inch of rock was formed.

Shallow seas continued to cover Iowa and deposit layers of limestone and fossils for many millions of years. Iowa was sub-tropical and very warm during these long periods. Parts of it resembled the great reefs seen today in south Florida and the Caribbean area, and large fossil beds were formed. Today, these rocks are quarried for a wide variety of purposes.

TRILOBITE

Shale is used to make brick and tile; gypsum is used for plaster and building board; and limestone is used for concrete. At times, the sea was very salty and couldn't support life. When conditions were favorable, some of the most numerous species were corals and sponges. Later on, fish became the main form of sea life. Numerous shark teeth and fish with bony skeletons are preserved as fossils. Most were small but some were as long as 25 feet.

CORAL-SPONGE UNDERWATER PRAIRIES

310 million years ago, Iowa lay near the edge of a shallow sea. The climate was tropical and great numbers of plants grew in the coastal forests and swamps. The seas rose and fell over the next 45 million years laying down numerous alternating layers of sandstone, limestone, shale, clay and siltstone. The most important geologic deposit of this era was

massive seams of coal in southern Iowa where the larger swamps and forests lay.

Coal is a burnable rock formed by the changing of decayed vegetation under pressure from rock layers that later formed above it. The formation of peat, partially decayed plants, is the first stage in the process. Peat is formed in poorly-drained coastal swamps. It is estimated that it took 10 feet of peat

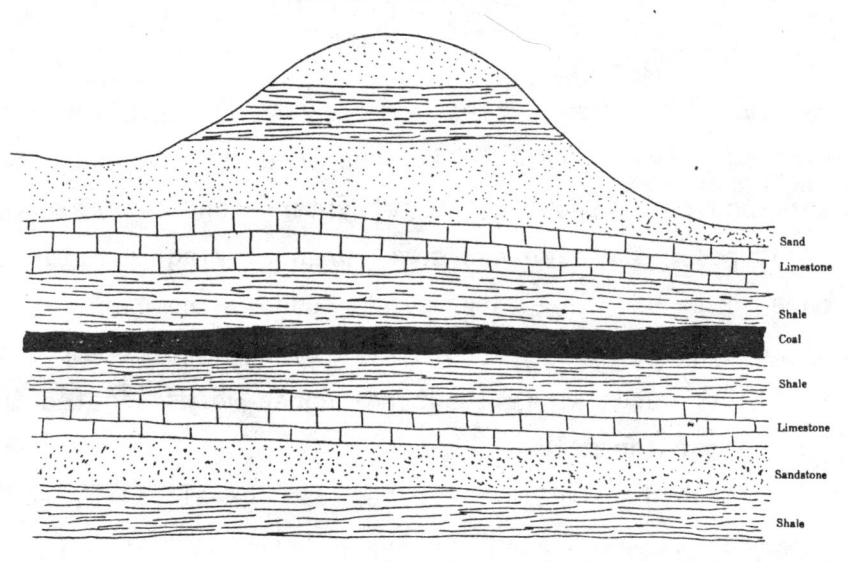

CHART SHOWING COAL SEAM

Sand
Limestone
Shale
Coal
Shale
Limestone
Sandstone
Shale

to produce 1 foot of coal. Some of the coal seams in Iowa today are hundreds of feet deep, and several feet thick. Tons and tons of plantlife died, and were concentrated into coal. What type of plants could grow this abundantly? The coal swamps grew jungles of sealy lycopod trees, tree ferns, cypress trees, palms and mangrove-like trees. A dense carpet of ferns and rushes covered the ground. The vegetation was as thick as any of today's jungles. Because of a year-round climate like that of the jungles of Africa, the plants grew thickly all year. Over millions of years, the plants yielded enough peat, and eventually coal, to enable Iowa to mine 9 million tons in the peak year of 1917.

By this time, strange creatures inhabited the lands and seas. Animal life had developed beyond the soft-bodied sponges, jellyfish and crab-like creatures. The time had come when living creatures came out of the water and found a home on land. Slimey snails moved sluggishly along the stems of leafless weeds while thousand-legged worms scooted in and out of the mold.

Fish had grown into species of great size, and some of them had acquired the ability to live briefly on land, where they preyed on the worms and snails. These animals, at home on land and sea, were called amphibians.

During the next 80 million years, there is an absence of rock records. Iowa was a low dry plain and erosion was the principal geologic process at work.

The age of dinosaurs saw northwestern Iowa covered by the last of the great inland seas. No dinosaur remains have yet been discovered in Iowa as they have been in the states to our west. However, some fossils of large sea reptiles have been found. One of the major rock formations dating from this period consists of the gypsum deposits found around Ft. Dodge. Gypsum is formed by the evaporation of sea water and the hardening of the salt it leaves behind. Gradually, the seas retreated, nearly to their present locations.

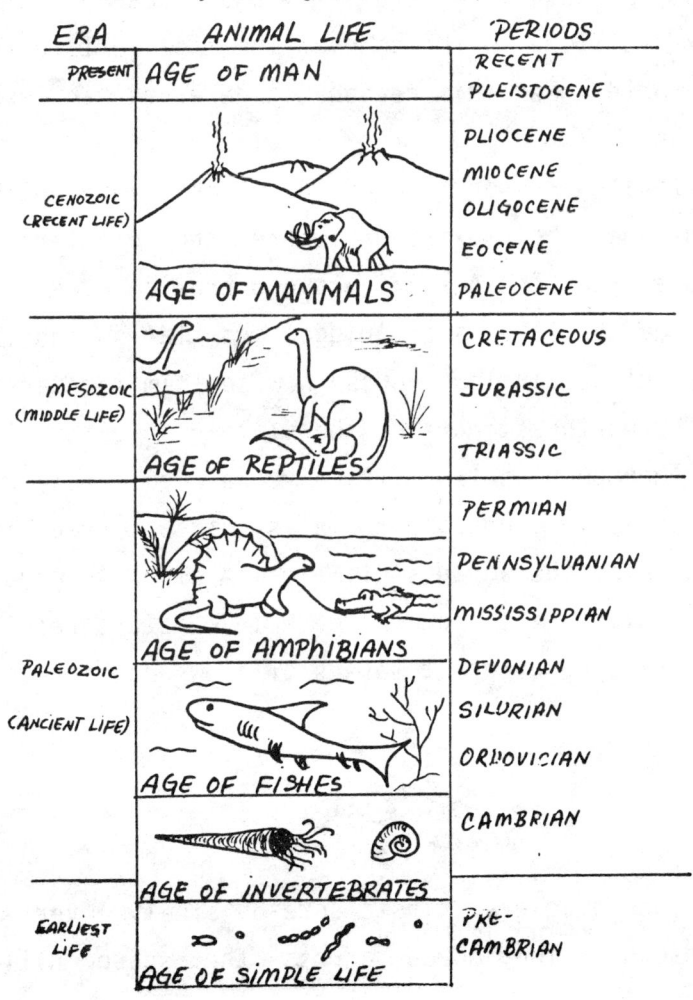

ERA	ANIMAL LIFE	PERIODS
PRESENT	AGE OF MAN	RECENT / PLEISTOCENE
CENOZOIC (RECENT LIFE)	AGE OF MAMMALS	PLIOCENE / MIOCENE / OLIGOCENE / EOCENE / PALEOCENE
MESOZOIC (MIDDLE LIFE)	AGE OF REPTILES	CRETACEOUS / JURASSIC / TRIASSIC
PALEOZOIC (ANCIENT LIFE)	AGE OF AMPHIBIANS / AGE OF FISHES / AGE OF INVERTEBRATES	PERMIAN / PENNSYLVANIAN / MISSISSIPPIAN / DEVONIAN / SILURIAN / ORDOVICIAN / CAMBRIAN
EARLIEST LIFE	AGE OF SIMPLE LIFE	PRE-CAMBRIAN

If we look at the history of the earth as taking place during one calendar year, the events that have been described have taken 364 days and 20 hours. On the scale of a year's time, the Ice Age, a most significant event in forming our state as we see it, took only 4 hours. It covered a real time span of about 2 million years. By comparison, only 5 minutes of geological time has elapsed since man first set foot in North America. The Ice Age was such a major event, because in a relatively short span of time it provided Iowa with some of the most fertile soil in the world. For this reason, it deserves an expanded discussion.

Iowa's present landscape looks very unlike the landscape that existed before the glaciers came. Before the Ice Age, rivers and erosion etched a land of steep valleys, sharp ridges and flat uplands. The only place in Iowa we can now see similar terrain is in the northeast part of the state.

Then perhaps two million years ago, for reasons not totally understood, a shift occurred in the balance of the world's climate. A slight decrease in temperature and an increase in moisture resulted in the building of great masses of snow and ice in the Arctic.

The glaciers first spread slowly over Iowa's landscape. They moved across the sharp hills and valleys shaped earlier, filling them in with the materials they carried, much like a modern bulldozer moves dirt and fills in land They scooped soil material, trapped rocks in their paths and carried them farther south. Much of this material was actually taken up and transported within the ice mass. Smaller rocks and boulders were ground down and turned into clay. They eventually came to rest against the existing surface, lodged there by advancing ice or left behind by melting ice. This ice-transported sediment is called till or boulder clay. Drift is a term sometimes used to refer to all of the deposits that came from glacial ice or its melted water. This blanket of glacial drift over Iowa varies in thickness from very little in parts of northeast Iowa to recorded depths of over 600 feet in west-central Iowa. From these masses, sheets of ice, perhaps thousands of feet thick, spread outward under their own weight and reached across the North American continent.

    A glacier itself might stretch for hundreds or thousands of miles and carry with it untold tons of materials. It didn't actually move as a unit. It did move outward under the added ice and stress of its own weight. When it got just so high, it started to flatten out much as stacked mud does. The blanket of ice at its thickest, may have been as much as 2 miles thick. The great weight actually caused the Earth's crust to sink. The glaciers advanced inch by inch very steadily, carrying material with them. A glacier would expand at a speed of about an inch a week.

11

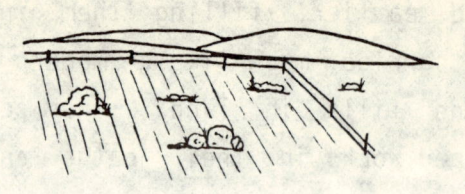

Farmers in some areas of Iowa occasionally must clear boulders from their fields only to find a season or two later that others have worked their way to the surface during winter's freeze and thaw. These boulders are called erratics because they originally came from Canada and Minnesota and are not native to Iowa. The presence of these worn and weathered erratics in Iowa provides additional evidence of the power of moving ice and the direction from which the glaciers came.

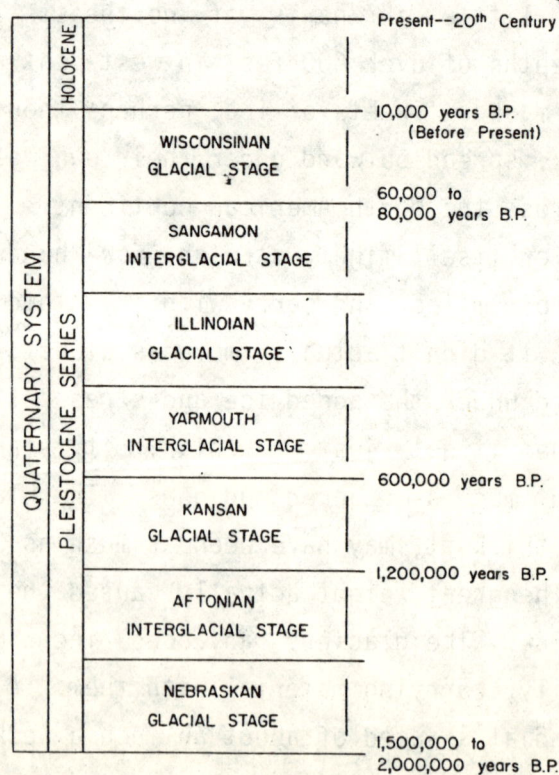

System	Series	Stage	Age
QUATERNARY SYSTEM		HOLOCENE	Present--20th Century
			10,000 years B.P. (Before Present)
	PLEISTOCENE SERIES	WISCONSINAN GLACIAL STAGE	
			60,000 to 80,000 years B.P.
		SANGAMON INTERGLACIAL STAGE	
		ILLINOIAN GLACIAL STAGE	
		YARMOUTH INTERGLACIAL STAGE	
			600,000 years B.P.
		KANSAN GLACIAL STAGE	
			1,200,000 years B.P.
		AFTONIAN INTERGLACIAL STAGE	
		NEBRASKAN GLACIAL STAGE	
			1,500,000 to 2,000,000 years B.P.

Where glacial drift has been eroded away, places can be seen where the bedrock underneath was planed and smoothed by the ice and its surface left very smooth and almost polished. Also, boulders and rocks were carried over the bedrock, gouging grooves of various sizes and depths into the rock surface. The rocks left tracings like you might leave by running your finger across wet clay. Our modern fertile soil is the weathered exterior of materials left by glacial action. In the thousands of years since the ice disappeared, weathering, plant growth, root systems, and burrowing organisms have all contributed to the changing of raw glacial deposits into the rich soils that we now know.

Rivers and their valleys also provide clues about Ice Age events. Consider the large rivers of Iowa. They were formed or enlarged during the Ice Ages. Their valleys are usually much broader than the river. Only during very major floods do we see them carry enough water to even fill their valleys. When the glaciers melted, these rivers carried enough water regularly to have created the huge valleys we now see. The Mississippi, for instance, would have constantly carried 10 times as much water as it does now. It was this volume of water and its eroding action that carved out the huge volume of dirt, silt and rock.

With the passing of thousands of years, the climate got warmer and the moisture became less. As a result, the ice began to thin and melt. Some ice probably stayed for many years in low, sheltered areas much like some winter snow can still be found in spring in rock crevices.

Iowa was partly or completely covered by glaciers many times. The four principal periods of ice cover, in order from the oldest to the youngest, are called the Nebraskan, Kansan, Illinoian and Wisconsinan glacial stages. They carry the names of the states

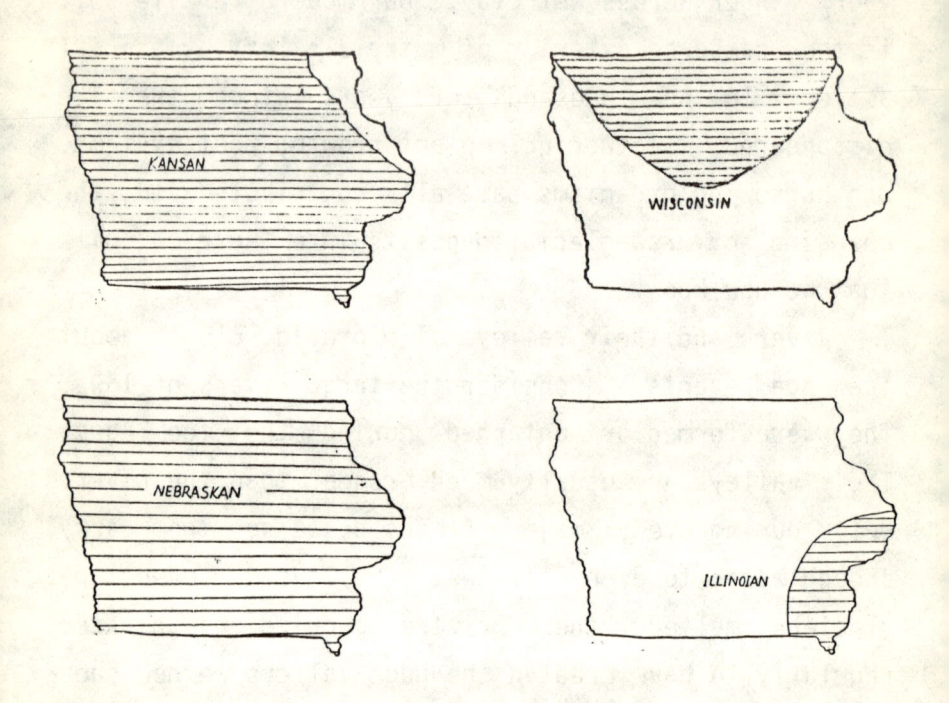

where their most easily recognized deposits occur. In between these periods of glaciation, the climate returned to conditions like we have now, and the land which the glaciers left was exposed to weathering, erosion and soil formation. Each glacier covered up and eliminated river valleys, changed others and created still others. They eroded and filled valleys and added many sediments to the land.

It is important to note that all of the earth materials deposited by glaciers, by streams that flowed from them, and by the winds that blew across the region are loose, not hardened like the rocks below. They are the materials in which crops grow and from which water can be drawn for drinking. Even when deep wells are used, some water taken out has trickled down through the sediments. A large part of Iowa's glacial drift has been covered with wind-deposited sediment called loess. Loess consists primarily of silt. These materials were first deposited by rivers or glacial meltwater, then were picked up by the wind and moved out across the landscape. The thickest accumulation of loess (100 feet or more) is near the Missouri river. The thickness tapers off the farther away one gets.

[Diagram showing layers: TOP SOIL, SILT / LOESS / DRIFT / BEDROCK]

Alluvium is another rich, sediment covering found within Iowa's principal valleys. It consists of material laid down by rivers and streams.

These glacial-age sediments also yield remains of plants and animals that inhabited Iowa during this period of geological history. The plant life of the Ice Age resembled that of Canada today. It consisted, at times, of closed pine forests, indicating the climate was cool. Apparently, the climate got even cooler, for the vegetation later changed to more widely separated spruce trees. These are cold weather trees that one would expect to find today in northern Canada. This is when Iowa was at its coldest point.

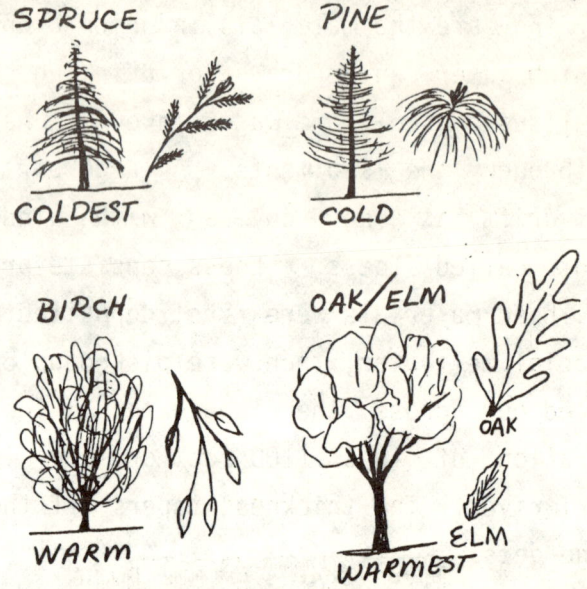

SPRUCE — COLDEST

PINE — COLD

BIRCH — WARM

OAK/ELM — WARMEST

As the climate got warmer because of changes in climate and the retreat of the glaciers, warmer weather trees and plants replaced cold weather ones. The plant life went from Spruce (coldest) to Pine (cold) to Birch (warm) to Oak and Elm (warmer). The way to tell warm weather trees from cold weather trees is the size and number of their leaves. The smaller the leaf, the colder the climate in which it can survive.

Iowa even became warmer and dryer than it is now, and the trees yielded to plants better adapted to dry climates--the prairie plants and grasses. About 3,000 years ago, oak trees began to come back. This change reflects a return to a slightly cooler and more moist climate. Judging from past climate records, some scientists feel that this change is the first indication of a very slow cooling that will start another Ice Age.

[Three maps of Iowa showing: ICE — 12,000 YEARS AGO; TUNDRA — 11,000 YEARS AGO; TALL GRASS — 10,000 YEARS AGO]

The animals that inhabited Iowa during the glacial age are varied. There are tiny white shells as well as large tusks and bones of woolly mammoths. These animals can be divided into 4 basic categories: 1) large extinct animals, with no direct descendents, such as the ground sloth, giant beaver, mastadon, wild pig, some oxen, and giant armadillo; 2) animals that are now extinct on this continent, but whose descendents survived on other continents. These would include horses, camels, llamas, and mammoths. It is not known why the animals in the first two

17

categories became extinct   3) Animals that still survive but are only found in the far north. These include musk ox, reindeer and many rodents.   4) The last group inhabited the state at least until historic times, and many of the smaller species still remain. Bison, moose, elk, bear, wolf, otter, foxes, coyotes, rabbits, deer, mice, beaver and squirrels are good examples.

Nearly 2 billion years of geologic change have been described. Some of the changes have been easily traced and can be easily seen. Others are almost impossible to see or trace. All of these events and processes make Iowa what it is today in terms of its height above sea level, position between rivers and natural resources. Now that we have looked at the geologic aspects of Iowa's history, we are ready to turn our attention to the relatively small span of time occupied by man that will make up the remainder of this book.

CHAPTER II

The first people in what is now the United States and Iowa were immigrants from Asia. They came across the Bering Strait about 30-40,000 years ago following herds of migrating animals. At this time, ice sheets covered much of North America. Because of the water trapped in the ice, sea level was much lower. More land was exposed between what is now Russia and Alaska. At the end of the Ice Age some 12,000 years ago, the "land bridge" disappeared. Those who were already here were cut off from the Old World, so they developed different cultures of their own. These immigrants kept moving south-easterly following the game animals.

Scraper   Bone Awl

Small groups of Indians, called bands, lived together and eventually developed their own language, clothing and customs. In many cases, bands over large areas were distinct but related to others in the region.

Our first real evidence of inhabitants in Iowa dates from about 12,000 years ago. It had taken about 20-30,000 years for the migration to reach Iowa. When they got here, ice covered the north-central part of the state. Beyond the ice there were patches of prairie, and forests of fir and spruce trees. The temperature was about 11 degrees cooler at the ice front.

During the next 11,000 years, the people changed very little physically, but went through many cultural changes. As new processes and inventions were introduced, the people who used them changed. Groups using the old ways were drawn into the more advanced group and became much like them.

The first people were called the Paleo Indians. The word "paleo" means old, and refers to the most ancient peoples on record. These people were hunters and didn't stay in one place for any length of time. They found shelter where they could in protected areas or natural rock shelters and overhangs (Paleo people did not have permanent shelters.) They followed the migratory Ice Age animals including giant bison, ancient horses, camels and elephants. To kill the animals, they stampeded them into gulleys or ran them into mud which served to trap the creatures. That way the animals could easily be killed. They used weapons such as spears, and torches to hunt, and had a variety of butchering tools designed for use after a kill was made. There was probably no warfare among related bands, so offensive weapons were not needed.

The amount of food they could gather influenced the size of the group. If food was abundant during all seasons, the group could be larger. Within the band, the Indians probably lived in small family groups much of the year. There were few people within the boundaries of the state. Each group would have its own territory and be lead by a male leader. Generally, bands within a region would be distinct, but related to the neighboring bands. There would be few difficulties due to trade and the fact that they would have to hunt together. Without this cooperation, the kill would have been much less successful.

A hunting culture needs a lot of territory and is constantly moving around. The ever-present need for fresh food didn't leave much time for fighting. However, hunters are known for having lots of time on their hands. These wanderers had no domesticated animals such as dogs or horses, nor did they have food animals such as cattle.

Clovis or Folsom Point

They used the spear, and are best known for their spear points called Clovis or Folsom points. The best known Paleo Indian site in Iowa is the Cherokee Sewer Site. There the deepest levels date to the late Paleo Indian Period (8500 years old). The site represents a place where bison were butchered and cooked, hides prepared and tools made. Towards the end of the Paleo period the huge sloths, elephants and other animals had gradually disappeared. Generally, the animals had become smaller and faster, so new hunting implements were invented. Some were used to cut the animals into usable parts.   Others were used to scrape and sew hides into clothing   Probably the most important invention was the atlatl or spear thrower. It was made of a piece of wood 15 to 30 inches long. At one end was a hand grip.   At the other was a hole or socket. The blunt end of a short spear was placed in this socket.   By using this extension of the arm, a spear could be thrown faster, farther and with more power than before   This invention became more important during the time the next culture appeared.

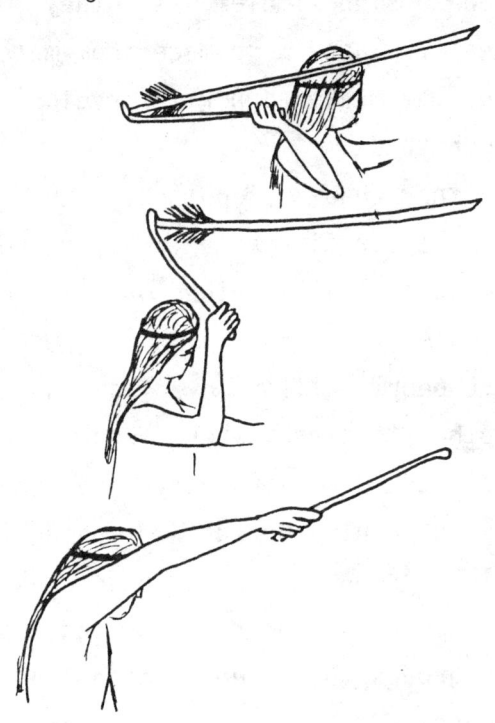

The Archaic, meaning "old", peoples replaced the Paleo Indians about 8,000 years ago. At this time, the climate of the Ice Age had given way to conditions that are warmer than the present day. The large Ice Age animals were gone, replaced with ones that are still found in Iowa today. The plants also changed with the climate and now there were many more new kinds of wild seeds and nuts on the prairies and in the hardwood forests to add to the Indians' diet. These new protein sources became increasingly important. The Archaic peoples relied more heavily on gathering the nuts, seeds, and berries. They also adapted tools such as hand stones and milling slabs to grind the seeds they collected.

In addition to stone implements, they used some copper implements. These were made from material that originated in the Lake Superior region which was obtained through trade.

Since they had no pottery, they probably heated stones in their fire pits to use in roasting or to drop into water-filled hides or woven baskets in order to boil water.

The Archaic people still moved around from one season to another to places where food was available. Each group had its own territory big enough that enabled them to hunt and gather enough to feed themselves. They probably saw few people except when trading with their neighbors. The Indians probably lived in small groups, built no permanent houses, had plenty to eat and waged very little, if any, warfare.

Three new ideas marked the change between the Archaic and Woodland periods. These were the use of pottery, the beginning of horticulture and new religious ideas and practices. The Woodland Indians appeared in Iowa about 2500 years ago. These people used pottery. They made it by rolling clay into a rope, then stacking one layer upon another. They used the pottery for storage as well as art. There were large villages in southeast Iowa where we have found evidence that they were trading for goods from as far away as the Rocky Mountains and the Gulf of Mexico. These people buried their dead in mounds and placed various objects in the mounds with the bodies.

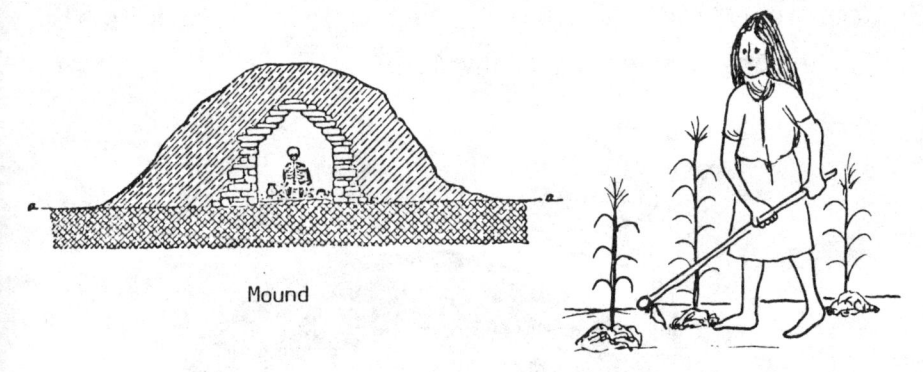

Mound

Mound Builder

Approximately 2000 years ago, the middle Woodland culture called "Hopewell" spread into eastern Iowa from Illinois and Ohio. It brought with it religious leaders and the building of large rounded burial mounds. People from many villages probably gathered to hold ceremonies and to bury their important dead. Indians placed bodies, bones or burned remains in log tombs or pits in the ground. Then dome-shaped mounds were built over the pits. With the burials were earspools, shells from the Gulf Coast, obsidian from the Rockies, copper from Lake Superior and many other objects not found close by. These objects were rarely found in villages. They were special burial items

25

that indicated the status of the person buried. The variety of items indicated a great amount of trading over wide distances. The number of people eligible to be buried in Hopewell mounds is not large, as apparently only important religious leaders merited the fancy and time-consuming treatment. Mounds are often located on low flat lands along main streams and are as high as 12 feet. The most elaborate structures are in Illinois and Ohio. A good Iowa example is the Toolesboro Mounds near Oakville.

Hopewell Wigwam

The Hopewell people lived in larger groups than earlier Indians and built fortified towns and wove cloth. The towns consisted of "wigwams" made of sheets of bark or woven mats of cattails that covered a frame of bendable saplings. The village itself was usually hidden in the edge of the forest. At the same time, they raised some garden crops. The Hopewell's village success was based on effective hunting and gathering.

MILL CREEK SITES X

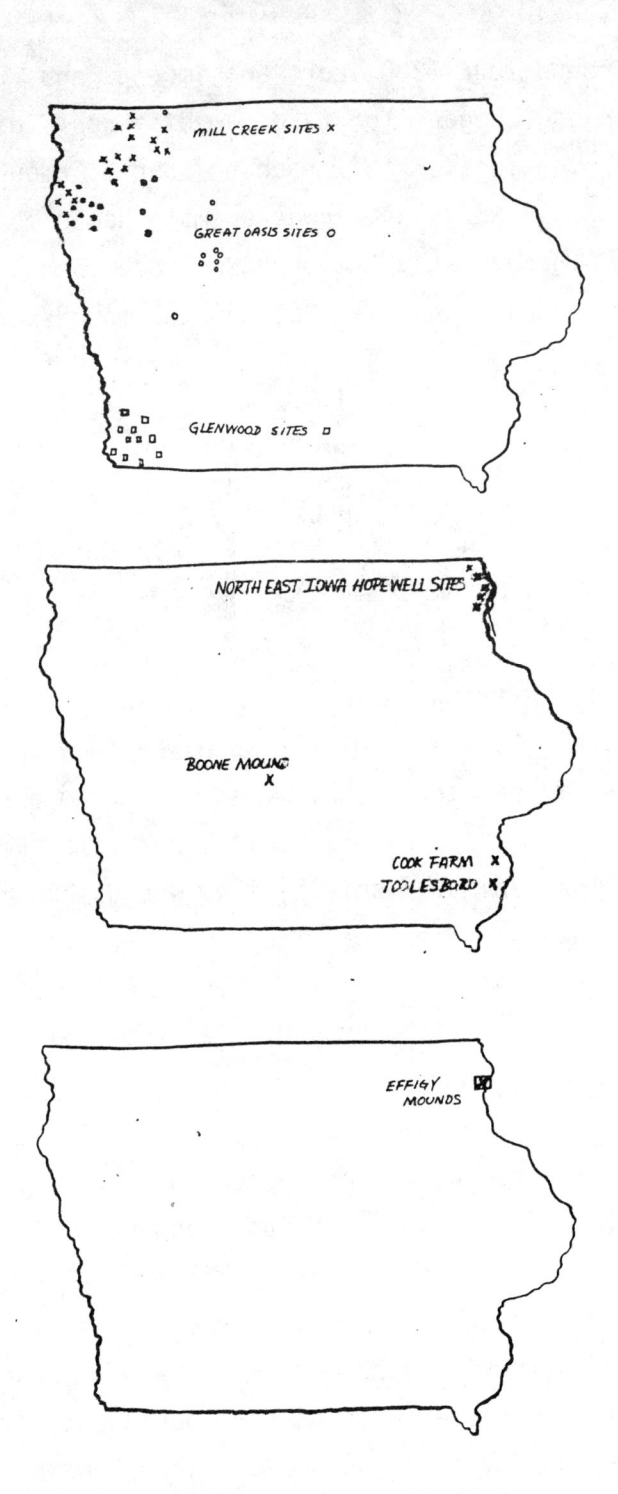

GREAT OASIS SITES O

GLENWOOD SITES □

NORTH EAST IOWA HOPEWELL SITES

BOONE MOUND
X

COOK FARM X
TOOLESBORO X

EFFIGY MOUNDS

27

Around Iowa 1200 years ago, mounds and religious ceremonies began to take a different direction. Smaller versions of the rounded burial mounds were built. In northeast Iowa, animal-shaped mounds were built. These "effigy" mounds included birds, bears, and other local animals. Most of the mounds were built

Mound Builder

by people carrying baskets of earth which was piled in one place. No one knows for sure why they were built, but we think that they resulted from a religious observance. These people felt that if they could honor the animal's spirit, they would take over some of its powers. Some of the most famous of these mounds are at the Turkey River Mound preserve near Millville, and Effigy Mounds (a National Monument) near Marquette.

One thousand years ago, the Indians in the Eastern United States were influenced by the cultures of Mexico. This influence became apparent in Western Iowa with the Great Oasis, Mill Creek and Glenwood cultures. These people were different from previous Indians as they were primarily farmers. Consequently, they stayed in one location more permanently than most Indians who followed the animals they hunted.

Great Oasis House

The Great Oasis people lived in western Iowa from 1100 to 700 years ago. They lived at the same time as the Glenwood, Mill Creek and Oneota cultures, and lived in villages that contained several rectangular houses. Each house was started in a shallow pit about 1 1/2 feet deep. The walls were built of vertical posts with sticks woven through them and covered with mud. The roof was a rounded grass thatch. They occupied the village in the winter, and either hunted or tended gardens in the summer. They were not overly influenced by outsiders, but did trade with the Mill Creek people.

These groups were the first to farm on a full-time basis. This enabled them to live in larger groups because they could rely on an adequate and steady food supply even if the winter and summer hunting did not go well. They were not at the total mercy of finding available supplies. They could raise their own food, know where to plant from year to year, and could judge how much they needed. Pottery was useful in cooking and storage, and was an important item in trade.

Even though crops provided the largest part of the Indians' diet, their gardens were small. They covered only two or three acres per family. The men cleared the ground by burning bushes and pulling out small trees, while the rest was done by the women.

Corn was planted as soon as the frost left the ground in the spring. Five to seven grains were placed in each hill. The hills were two or three feet apart. Beans were planted a month later in the same hill so the plants could climb the cornstalk.

Corn was the most important food and was fixed in many ways. Small young stalks provided a sap or syrup and were then eaten. The full grown ears were roasted over hot coals as they came from the plant. Most of the corn was then stored in pits so it could be used through the winter.

The evidence of these Mill Creek people consists of the remains of large, rectangular earth lodges dug into the ground. The roof and sides were supported by poles and probably covered by a grass thatch. The walls were plastered with mud. A central fireplace was the main feature. They both hunted animals with the bow and arrow and grew crops consisting of corn, beans, sunflower and squash.

Mill Creek Earth Lodge

The Mill Creek people lived in fortified villages which were often surrounded by a wooden stockade or moat. This indicated they were bothered by raids from hostile neighbors. These were occupied during the winter, and the tribe left to hunt buffalo during the summer. Evidence of these people has been found on the Big and Little Sioux rivers in northwestern Iowa.

The Glenwood culture lived at the same time as the other two cultures in scattered earthlodge villages near present-day Glenwood. They apparently traded with another group called the Oneota. The Mill Creek and Glenwood peoples were forced out of Iowa about 700 years ago by a combination of the changing climate and the hostile Oneota Indians.

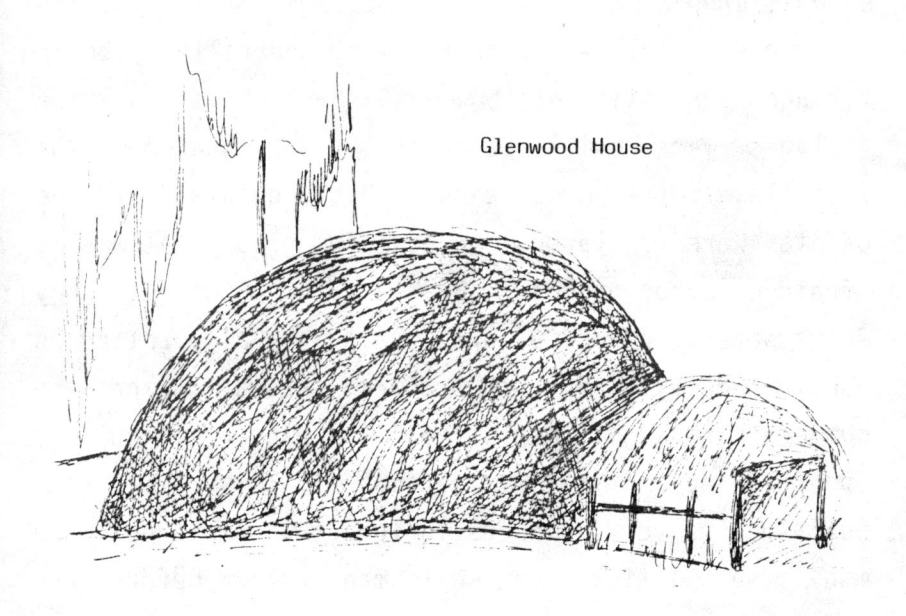

Glenwood House

Oneota Longhouse

At the same time that the Mill Creek, Great Oasis and Glenwood people lived in their limited areas (1000 A.D.), the Oneota lived throughout the state. They relied primarily on forest hunting and to a lesser extent, crop raising. They roamed most of the year as they had to follow the game. They generally lived in villages consisting of about 50 bark huts. These villages were built permanently and located on the floodplains of major streams. This suggests that the Oneota were a large and powerful group that wasn't afraid of other groups. In fact, we suspect they drove several other cultures out. They also relied on hunting buffalo and the crops raised during the summer. These got them through the winter, which they spent in their villages. Through all this time, the buffalo were very numerous in Iowa. It would not take many years after the white man arrived before they would be driven out and hunted until there were none left.

Over the next 300 years, the three Indian cultures disappeared; having been pushed out, destroyed or taken in by other more numerous or advanced tribes. These tribes had in turn been pushed out or had moved seeking better hunting grounds. The Oneota had Iowa to themselves from about 1300 A.D. until they were pushed out by an 1830 treaty. As their culture changed, they became what we know as the Ioway. In fact, nearly all the Indians in Iowa at the time of the first white men, except the Ioway, were tribes pushed west by other displaced tribes.

YEARS AGO	INHABITANTS
11,000	PALEOLITHIC PEOPLE
5,000	ARCHAIC PEOPLE
2,500	WOODLAND INDIAN
2,000	HOPEWELL INDIAN
1,100	GLENWOOD MILL CREEK ONEOTA GREAT OASIS

INDIANS AFTER 1200 A.D. WERE OF THE 50 SOUIX RELATED OR 70 ALGONQUIN RELATED

A good example of this occurred over the last 400 years. The Oneota were established, but were replaced by or changed into the Ioways. The Ioways were forced

33

to share their hunting grounds by the Sauk and Mesquakie who had been driven out of Wisconsin and Michigan by the French.

The Indians who ranged in Iowa when the white man arrived were of two groups: the 50 Dakota or Sioux-related tribes such as the Ioway, Osage, Oto and others who originally came from the west. The second group was the Algonquin tribes such as the Sauk and Mesquakie who had at one time lived farther east. The difference in culture between Sioux and Algonquin were the main factors in the division of tribes.

IOWA WAS PRIMARILY ALGONQUIAN LANGUAGE GROUP
ONEOTA AND HOPEWELL CULTURE

There were a few thousand Indians living permanently in Iowa before the Louisiana Purchase of 1804. Although the exact number of tribes that have inhabited Iowa during its entire history is not known, at least 17 different ones have lived within the confines of the present state boundaries. It was used mainly as a hunting ground by many tribes. The tribes

34

that did live here, held a seasonal hunt and lived on the meat and on crops raised during the summer. It is estimated that there were about 8,000 Indians roaming through Iowa. Of these 8,000, about 3,000 were Sauk or Mesquakies. However, each full tribe very seldom got together as a group. Even the allied Sauk and Mesquakie lived as neighbors, but as separate tribes. Each was further divided into sub-tribes. Thus the Illinois Indians who met Joliet had been driven temporarily across the river by the Iraquois. So, too, the Miami Indians who in 1690 begged Nicholas Pierrot to help them mine lead, had been pushed westward by these same warlike neighbors. Only the Ioway Indians are known to have been associated for a long time with the state that bears their name, maintaining a permanent residence in the area for 1000 years.

    A tribe would consist of a number of small villages made up of several families. In other words, the Ioway tribe might consist of seven groups roaming freely through a portion of the state. They would unite only in a major dispute with another tribe or for a large festival. This is much like saying your entire family is all related but live separately in different cities with their closest family members. You get together in times of tragedy, holidays or family reunions.

All the major tribes, such as the Sioux and Sauk, were in competition over hunting grounds. The outskirts of their hunting territories overlapped. There were no markers to separate territories. If a hunting party was out and happened on a smaller hostile party, they forgot the hunt and attempted to wipe their rivals out. The tribes were not strangers to each other. Sometimes they became allies to raid other tribes. After the immediate danger was over, close cooperation would also cease.

This became so frequent and costly that many tribes informally got together in southwest Iowa and declared it a neutral ground that all could hunt without fear of being attacked. This and trading are two of the instances of cooperation among tribes in

Iowa Later in history, there was an imitation of this in northeast Iowa which separated the Sioux from the Sauk and Mesquakie, both deadly enemies. The federal government started and unsuccessfully policed this neutral zone.

It was this frequent minor fighting and division among tribes that spelled their doom at the hands of the much more numerous and more technically advanced group of Europeans and their civilization.

We've seen in this chapter that starting 12,000 years ago Indians lived in Iowa. Each group was replaced by a more technologically and socially advanced group. The earlier peoples gradually developed into the later peoples with the help of new ideas developed beyond the region.

CHAPTER III

In the last chapter, we learned that the Indian tribes in Iowa both hunted and farmed. They spent time fighting each other and keeping old hatreds alive. There were not many of them and they roamed over large areas to hunt. As a result of this and other conflicts they found it impossible to unite for any length of time.

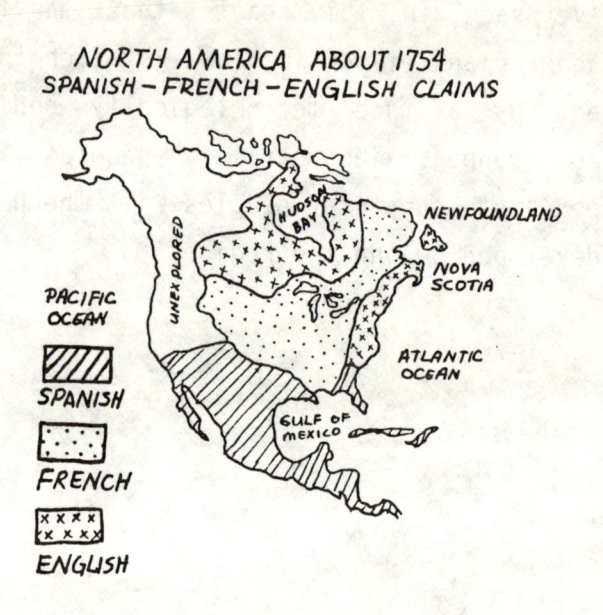

NORTH AMERICA ABOUT 1754
SPANISH - FRENCH - ENGLISH CLAIMS

SPANISH
FRENCH
ENGLISH

At the same time Europeans from France, England and Spain dominated exploration and colonization. By 1673 these 3 groups had established settlements on the North American continent along the East coast, in present day Florida and in the North and Southwest. These European nations began competing for control of this land especially when the land areas they wanted overlapped.

38

The British government was primarily interested in colonies to provide a market for goods as well as a source of raw materials. They had established permanent agricultural colonies along the Atlantic coast.

The French were interested in control of the fur trade. They established settlements to help the trade in what is now Canada. New Orleans was also owned by the French.

The Spanish were primarily interested in gold and silver. They established settlements in Mexico, the Southwest and Florida.

In 1673, two Frenchmen, Louis Joliet and Father Jacques Marquette led an expedition of seven people to explore the Mississippi. On June 25, 1673, these men came ashore at the mouth of what is now called the Iowa River near present day Toolesboro.

Joliet and Marquette were sent south from Quebec by the French governor there. Joliet was searching for a potential source of furs, new territories for France, and a possible northwest passage. Father Marquette accompanied him as a translator as well as a priest to teach the Catholic faith to the Indians.

The French were moving westward to establish fur trade as they had been forced out of the east by the British and Iraquois. West was the only safe way they could expand.

The explorers had heard about a great river from the Indians who warned them of huge river monsters.

Marquette and Joliet's Route

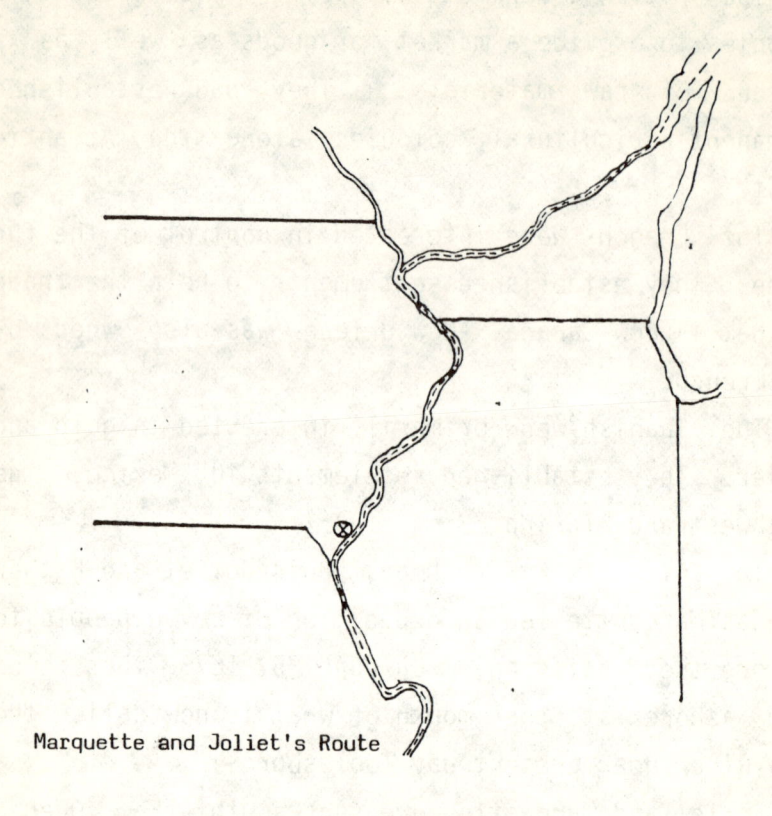

As they traveled down the river, they kept an alert eye out for these monsters. They didn't know what they would encounter on land either, so they camped each night in their canoes.

They traveled down the Wisconsin River, and on June 17, 1673, they floated out onto a wider river where they saw "a large chain of very high mountains." They were actually describing 300 foot bluffs along the Mississippi River where McGregor is today. On June 25, 1673, they spotted footprints and a path on the western side. They decided to follow the path hoping to find the people who had made the footprints.

The two explorers walked a distance inland and found a village of Illini Indians. The explorers called out so that the natives would not be startled by their presence. The Indians welcomed and entertained them overnight. As a sign of respect, the Indians gave the explorers a chief's son and escorted them for a distance as they proceeded down the river.

Joliet and Marquette

Joliet and Marquette eventually traveled south as far as the Arkansas River before returning to Quebec. This trip, and a later one by Robert Cavelier, Sieur de La Salle in 1682, resulted in all lands west of the Mississippi, including what we know as Iowa, being claimed by France.

After the explorers claimed the Mississippi River Valley, the French worked to keep their claim on this area. A small but courageous force of men--fur traders and miners, soldiers and priests fanned out through the Upper Mississippi Valley.

Indians guided French trappers and explorers along the best portage paths.

    The earliest explorers after Marquette whose names have come down to us were Pierre Charles Le Seur and Pierre Charlevoix. They explored the central and southeast portions of present day Iowa in the course of their fur trading.

    Nicholas Perrot was another of these traders. By 1685, he had a large fur trade business at Prairie du Chien (in future Wisconsin) and was trusted by the Indians. The Miami Indians had located lead deposits at the mouth of the Iowa River, but their mining methods weren't very good. They asked Perrot to advise them and run the mines. He did supervise the setting up of the smelters, but didn't stay long. His account of the fur trade and the Indians of the Upper Mississippi Valley is very valuable as it showed the lives of the Indians before the white man came in great numbers.

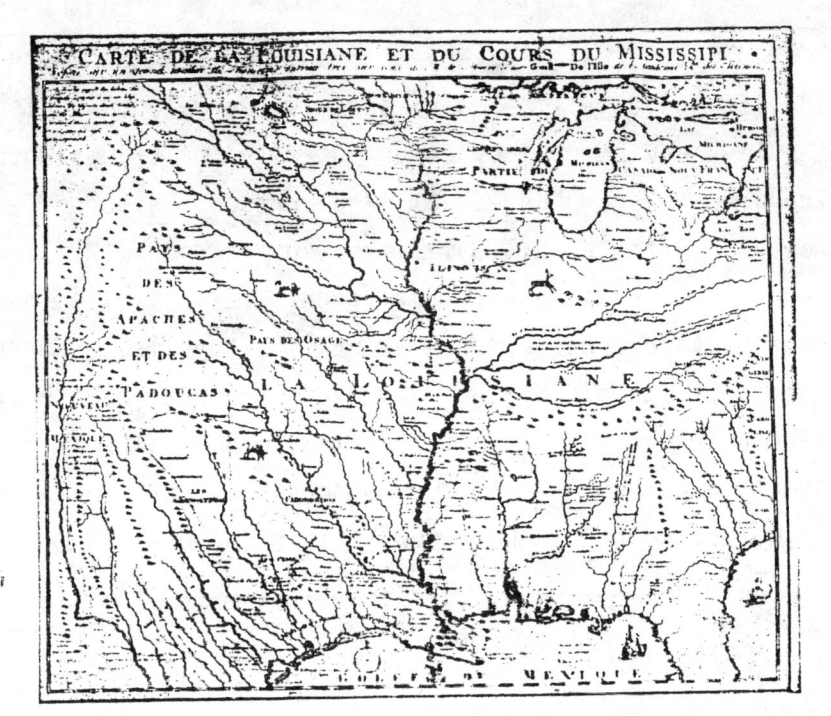

More was learned about the future Iowa because of the map drawn by William Delisle in 1718 that showed the Iowa rivers and the Chemin des Voyageurs or road of the (fur) traders. In addition, Pierre Paul Marin erected a military and fur post in what is now Clayton County in 1738--70 years before the Americans erected their Fort Madison.

Exploration, trading and fur trapping went well for a time, but, as more whites mingled with the Indians and used their hunting grounds, trouble was inevitable. The Sauk and Fox had united to avoid being destroyed singly by the Sioux and Chippewa. The Fox tribe had been greatly weakened by years of fighting with the French over the fur trade. The Fox were one of the few tribes that did not have good relations with the traders.

In 1735, Major De Noyelles and 250 men (84 French and 166 Indian allies) were sent to pursue and punish the Sauk and Fox. They caught up with the tribes when they found 55 lodges at the present site of Des Moines. After an all-day fight, 40 years to the day before the Battle of Lexington, very little had happened and a parley was called. De Noyelles ordered the tribes to disband or he would come back with a larger army and totally destroy them. The tribes didn't break their alliance, however, for fear of being destroyed by their powerful Indian enemies.

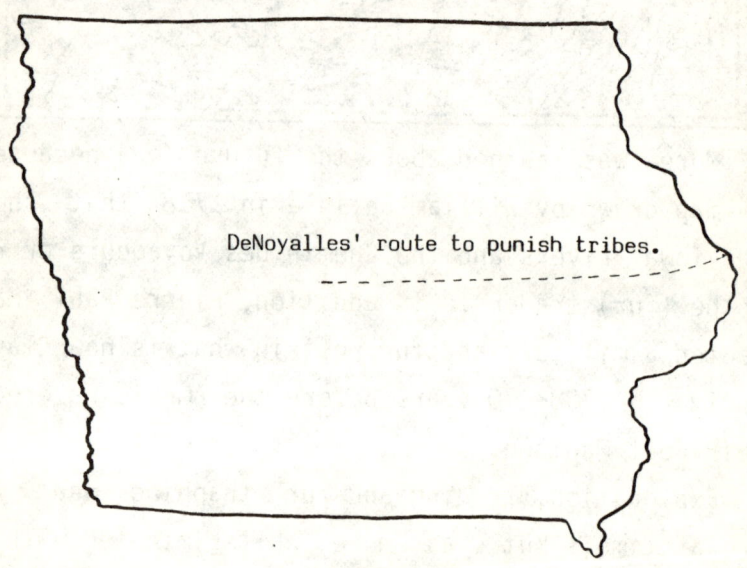

DeNoyalles' route to punish tribes.

The Mesquakie tribe was referred to as the Fox or Reynards by the French. In an early meeting between the two groups, the French asked a band of Mesquakies who they were. The Mesquakies replied giving the name of their band, the Fox, rather than their tribal name. The name stayed with the tribe and the French and others continued to refer to the entire tribe as the

Fox. In referring to them further in this book, the tribe will be referred to by their proper name - the Mesquakie.

When the fur trading or settlement interests of France, England or Spain brought them into competition for resources in the same area, conflicts erupted. One of these conflicts was the French and Indian War. Britain and France both wanted control of the Ohio River valley and the fur trade.

The land we now call Iowa was not directly involved in the French and Indian War, although some Indians and traders probably helped the French farther north. Iowa was affected though. When it looked as though the French would lose, they didn't want the Mississippi Valley falling into the hands of the British. Therefore they gave it to Spain with the understanding that it would be returned by 1800.

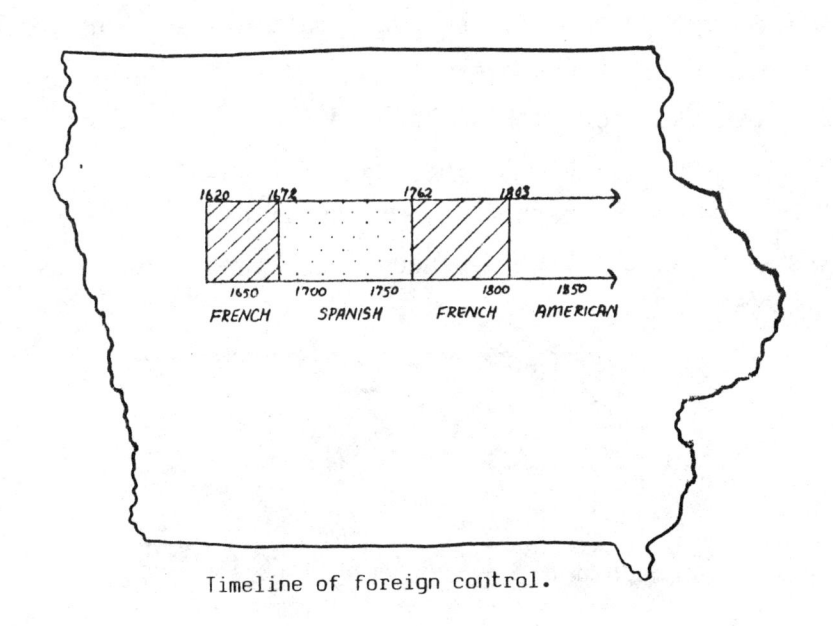

Timeline of foreign control.

The British eventually won the war in 1763, leaving England and Spain in control of the New World. The future Iowa had become part of the Spanish empire as a direct result of a war that was totally started and mostly fought by Europeans. The French period of ownership had lasted from 1673 to 1762.

Fur trading was the main industry in the Upper Mississippi Valley and the French were the leaders. One hundred thirty French-Canadians moved over the trails from Prairie du Chien to Spirit Lake and the Missouri River. These traders made calls on the Indians and traded manufactured goods for furs before returning to their home base. These men were not always honest or good businessmen. A raid by hostile whites or Indians, a change in prices or a tipped canoe could spell the difference between a successful trip, 6 months long, and a disaster. If the trader did manage to do well, he could multiply his original investment 10 times over.

Because of this great profit, traders did everything possible to encourage the Indians to trap for the furs rather than to survive. The Europeans were almost totally dependent on the tribes as a source for furs.

French settlers were often fur trappers and traders.

The traders bought trade goods such as knives, guns, ammunition, beads, cloth and iron utensils from companies on credit, then traded these items for pelts Before the Europeans came, the Indians knew how to get all the things they needed. By engaging in the trade, Indian people gradually lost their independent ways and became dependent on European goods for survival.

Before the Europeans, Indian people hand-made everything they needed from available materials. Indians soon found out, for instance, that a bone knife that took hours or days to make could be made of steel and obtained for pelts which were easy for him to trap. A steel knife would last longer and be much stronger than the one made of bone. As a result, the Indians started to desire more and more manufactured articles. This changed their traditional ways of doing things. Instead of occasionally trapping for food, they now trapped more often for pelts which would be exchanged for goods. Their territories had to be expanded to pursue the game The tribes gradually lost their self-reliance, customs and way of life.

Also, because of their trading alliances, each tribe became attached to a European nation; either Spain, France or England. Most Iowa Indians were loyal first to France and later to Britain. They were also becoming entangled in the Europeans' rivalries and wars. This, tied in with their already existing hatreds and search for new trapping grounds, was

47

keeping the tribes in a constant state of warfare. In many cases, Indians were used as troops against other countries and their Indian allies.

So we have learned that Iowa was explored by Marquette and Joliet and the Indian way of life was changed by the trappers. We also learned this area was affected by the events and European rivalries happening half a continent or half a world away. Iowa waited now for settlers to use the rich mineral, agricultural and natural resources.

CHAPTER IV

We saw in the last chapter that the land we now call Iowa had been explored by Joliet and Marquette and others. Interest in the fur-rich area continued.

The American revolution had been fought and the Americans now controlled the territory east of the Mississippi. In 1783, the United States and Spain faced each other across the Mississippi. The British controlled the northern area.

The Spanish did not move troops or people into the territory because of the high cost of building and maintaining military posts in a frontier area. Fearing that the Americans and British might push into their territory, the Spanish tried to strengthen their weak position by recruiting French traders friendly to the Indians. The Spanish gave these traders land grants to establish settlements, mines and fur posts. The most successful of these people was Julien Dubuque.

Courtesy Des Moines Register
JULIEN DUBUQUE

Julien Dubuque, a French-Canadian, had come from Prairie Du Chien in the 1780's when he learned of the rich lead deposits in what is now Dubuque and Jackson counties. Whether Dubuque was a saint or a sinner depends on who is telling the story. He did use the best technology of the times. It is said that he visited the Mesquakie Indians from time to time over several years and each time gave them rich gifts. Even so, the Mesquakie Indians and their leader, Kettle Chief, refused to allow him to open a mine. Finally, he threatened to set Catfish Creek on fire if they didn't. As he spoke, a helper was pouring oil in the creek, which was flowing in the direction of the pow-wow. At a signal, it was set on fire and the Indians, awed by his power, agreed that a mine wouldn't be a bad idea after all. This occurred in 1788.

When the Spanish became owner of Louisiana, Dubuque quickly got a land grant from the Spanish governor and called his operation "The Mines of Spain." This was in 1796. Soon, the first permanent settlement in future Iowa was an active mining center with smelting pits and furnaces, trading posts, cabins, barns and an Indian village. All of these things were complete with a cannon high up on the bluff.

Dubuque did a thriving business in lead and furs. He died in debt, but kept his good reputation among the Indians. After he died, they refused to let any other whites farm, trade or mine there.

Wintering Post

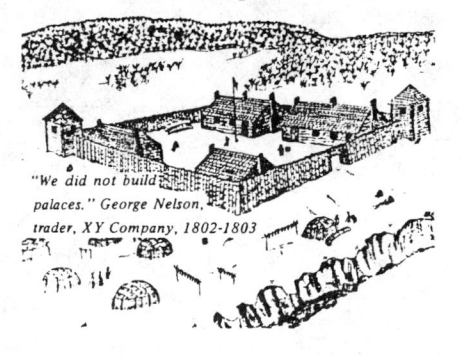

"We did not build palaces." George Nelson, trader, XY Company, 1802-1803

Another of the grants was 5,760 acres given to Basil Giard in 1795. It included land where the towns of Marquette and McGregor now stand.

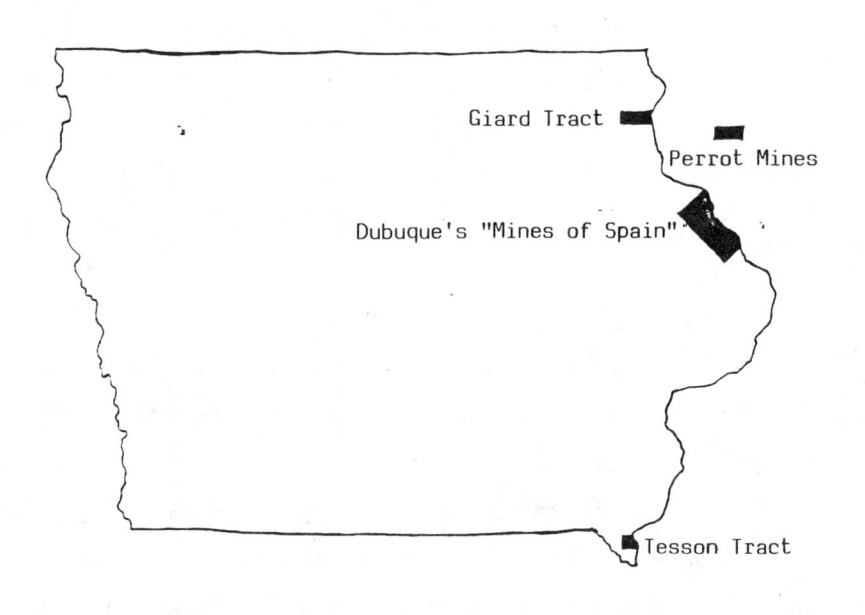

Giard Tract
Perrot Mines
Dubuque's "Mines of Spain"
Tesson Tract

In 1799, the Spanish awarded Louis Honore Tesson a grant of 6,000 acres at the head of the rapids of the Mississippi River to establish a fur trading post and keep the Indians friendly. As part of the initial agreement, Tesson planted an apple orchard to supplement his income. It was very popular with the tribes. Even though his business failed, the orchard survived and was frequently visited by Indians for many years.

The region was still held by Spain until 1800 when Spain, fearing that the United States might invade New Orleans, traded Louisiana to the now powerful France, ruled by Napoleon.

The French, however, had become deeply involved in a losing game of European politics and warfare and could not afford to defend or control Louisiana. Napoleon chose to sell all of Louisiana to the United States to prevent the British from occupying it and to raise money to keep the European war alive. At the same time, the new American nation wanted free trade in the port of New Orleans. The Spanish had closed the port and so had hurt American merchants. Jefferson was afraid the French would also close it. If this happened, the Americans would become dependent on the British. Jefferson offered to buy the port for 2 million dollars. He was prepared to offer 10 million. Under those circumstances, Emperor Napoleon took a hand in Iowa's history and changed its destiny. He said if the U. S. wanted the port, they also had to buy the entire Louisiana territory for 15 million dollars. President Jefferson knew a bargain when he saw it. He bought the entire territory for what amounted to less than 5 cents an acre. Thus,

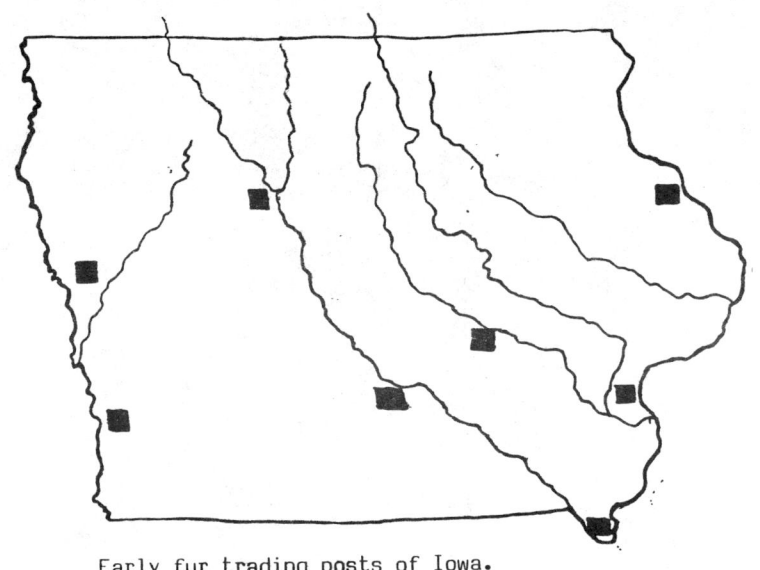

Early fur trading posts of Iowa.

On March 9, 1804, the future Iowa became part of the United States after 130 years under French and Spanish rule.

Aside from a few French traders, nobody knew anything about the vast new lands. They didn't know who really lived there or what the territory was good for. For many years, Thomas Jefferson had dreamed of and planned for an exploration of the land west of the Mississippi River. He immediately ordered an expedition to explore the Louisiana Purchase. Meriwether Lewis and William Clark were chosen as leaders. They were told to study the region's wild life, natural resources and inhabitants. Plans included a journey all the way to the Pacific Ocean. Jefferson wanted Lewis to claim Oregon for the U. S.

53

Lewis and Clark arrived at present-day Council Bluffs in August 1804.

On this trip they spent 33 days in the area that is now Iowa. They wrote of Iowa, "We camped at one of the most beautiful prairies we ever saw." On the western side of the Missouri, near the future site of Council Bluffs, they held council with the Oto and Missouri tribes and exchanged roast meat for some native watermelons.

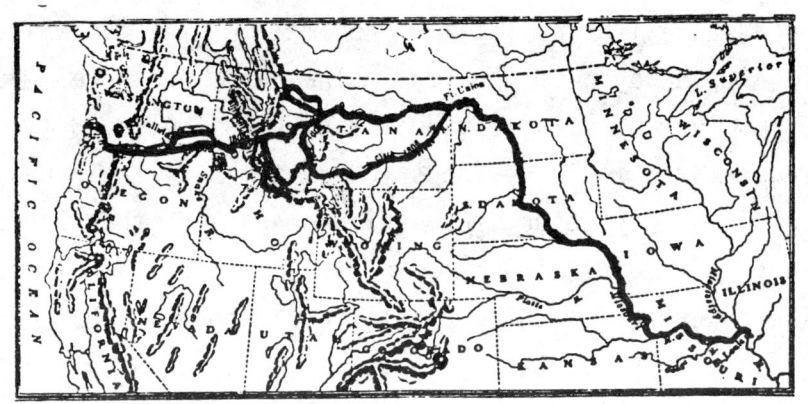

The Lewis and Clark Route.

Courtesy, Annals of Iowa

As they moved up the Missouri, Sgt. Charles Floyd died, apparently of a ruptured appendix. He was buried on the bluffs below the present city of Sioux City. The burial site is marked today by a monument to the only death during the expedition and the first white burial.

Hardly had the Lewis and Clark expedition set out, when President Jefferson instructed them to sign

Floyd Monument south of Sioux City, Iowa near Interstate 29

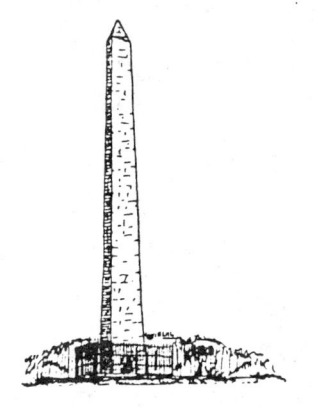

55

treaties with the Indians they met to give the whites legal ownership of the land. The President believed strongly in obtaining what the whites believed to be legal title to those lands. Many times in their haste to do so they tended to overlook many of the Indian ways of doing things, in favor of their own ideas. There were a few white people who thought that the Indian people, through education and religion, could live in a white society. However, most settlers considered the Indians people to be used for their own gain or as competitors for the land.

The first of these treaties that affected Iowa was in 1804. At that time, four Sauk braves killed three whites and some Osage Indians who were trespassing on their hunting grounds in what is now Iowa.

To the Indian way of thinking, protecting their hunting ground was just normal procedure. But the commander at St. Louis ordered that the Sauk and Mesquakie send their chiefs to answer for what they considered a crime. The whites saw this as a serious offense and also as an opportunity to make some land gains. Not wishing to meet the American troops, some Indians showed up. The whites never understood that each sub-tribe had several leaders who rose to power by proving their ability and leadership. They led various activities, but no single chief could make all decisions. In fact, they had no concept of chiefs as we have come to know them. These were chiefs who inherited the title, but they were only social rulers, much like modern kings who have very little political power   The leaders of one village had no power over any other groups. They also had no concept that land could be owned by an individual. Only things that could be moved could be sold. They believed that the land was owned only by the Great Spirit. If they were forced off by another tribe, that was simply his will.

LAND SIGNED BY SAC AND FOX INDIANS IN 1804

The Indians saw the meeting as a formality and no major leaders were there. The Indians thought the whites were crazy when they were asked to sell lands that only the Great Spirit owned. To humor the whites and gain the rich rewards they promised, they signed the treaty and started on a two-day drunk. However, when the spokesmen returned to their tribes and explained what they had done, their fellow tribesmen were not happy with the results.

The treaty said the tribes gave up all claims to lands east of the Mississippi. This included the largest Sauk village called Saukenuk across from the present site of Davenport. The tribe, however, was allowed to stay until the United States government told them to leave.

Black Hawk, the war leader of Saukenuk, argued that he knew nothing of the treaty, although he had signed treaties that confirmed it in 1816, 1822, and 1825. Perhaps he knew what he was signing, perhaps he didn't. At any rate, the Indians required decisions of this type to be made in council, as the entire tribe had to approve. The Americans' method of government decision-making differed from that of the Indians.

Pike's Route

President Jefferson was very interested in the Upper Mississippi region that includes the state of Iowa. In 1805, Zebulon Pike began an expedition to explore that area. Pike's orders required him to follow the river to its source and inform the inhabitants that the Americans were the owners. Pike also looked for fort sites and checked the moves of British traders.

Poling a keelboat upstream

With 20 men in a keelboat, the party journeyed up the Mississippi River from St. Louis. They stopped at the future locations of Fort Madison and Burlington. Pike spent time at and was impressed with Julien Dubuque's mines and settlement.

Zebulon Pike in the uniform of an officer of the War of 1812.

Farther north Pike was very impressed with the same bluffs that had attracted Joliet. They were named Pike's Peak many years before a mountain peak in Colorado qualified for the same name. Pike's expedition in 1805 marks the end of the period of exploration in Iowa history.

We have seen that in the late 1700's and early years of the 1800's, Iowa country was ruled by Spain, France and the United States. Such famous people as Jefferson, Lewis and Clark, Napoleon, Black Hawk and Zebulon Pike influenced the course of history of the region. And people like Julien Dubuque and Louis Honore Tesson were shaping the future course of events in Iowa. It was now open to the coming of new American influences.

CHAPTER V

We saw in the last unit that such famous people as Napoleon, Jefferson, Lewis and Clark, Black Hawk and Zebulon Pike were indirectly shaping Iowa's history and future. At the same time, people such as Dubuque and Tesson were trapping and mining in the wild country. It waited now for permanent settlers to use the rich mineral, agricultural and natural resources.

In 1808, the first American fort and trading post in Iowa was built: Ft. Madison. The government built the fort and trading post to discourage the British from trading with the Indians.

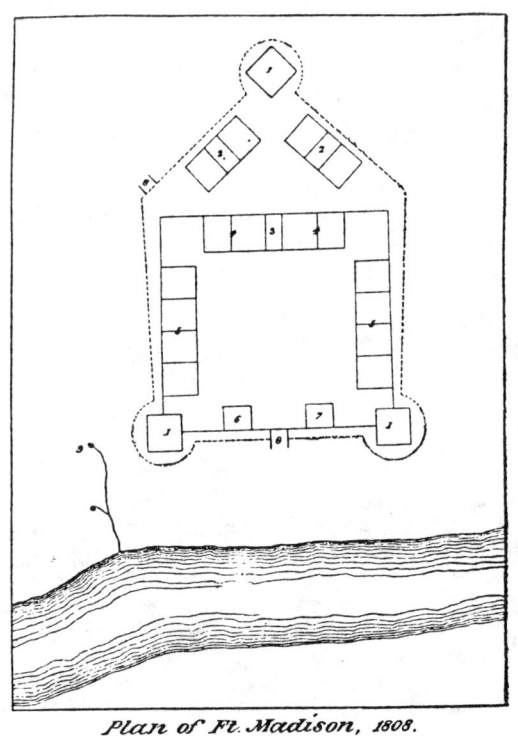

Plan of Ft. Madison, 1808.

1 Block Houses.   4 Officers Quarters.   7 Surgeons Office
2 Factory   5 Barracks   8 Gates
3 Passage-way   6 Guard-house   9 Spring

61

As relations between the British and the Americans became worse, the British encouraged the Sauk and Winnebago to attack the Americans. British agents and traders constantly told the Indians that the Americans were not to be trusted. The fact that the Americans acted like they were in hostile territory while building Ft. Madison and the fact that the Indians had little positive experience with them fueled the fire.

When the War of 1812 broke out, the Sauk actively helped the British, who, in return, supplied them with weapons. The Sauk had heard about the conflicts in the east, and knew of the results.

While the War of 1812 is remembered mainly for its land and sea battles on the Atlantic and southern coasts, few people realize that the Mississippi River Valley was also the scene of some important action.

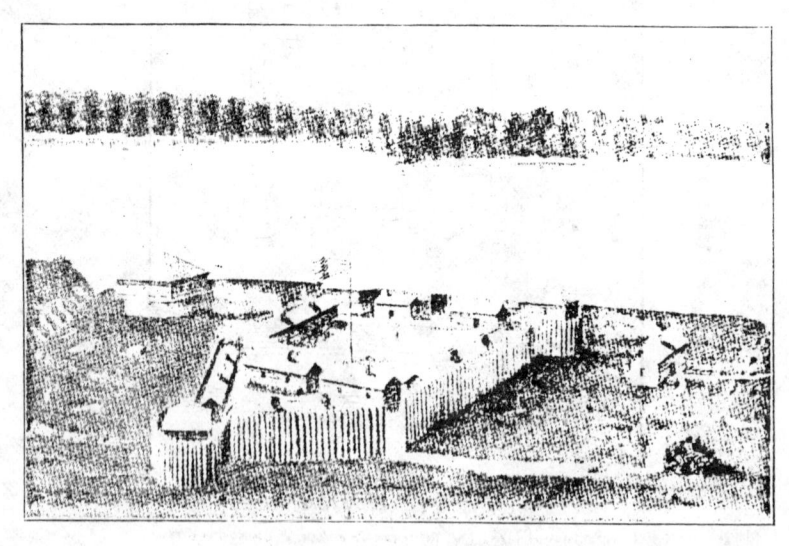

OLD FORT MADISON
Built in 1808

The poorly placed Ft. Madison was the only American fort north of St. Louis at that time. The Indians had been sniping at the fort for two years. Black Hawk led an attack on the fort in 1812. The siege lasted until 1813, when the American soldiers ran out of food and ammunition. The soldiers dug a tunnel to the river and escaped before setting fire to the fort.

The War of 1812 had come to Iowa. In 1814, Lt. Campbell and three gunboats of troops, intended as reinforcements for Ft. Shelby at Prairie Du Chien, Wisconsin, ran aground near the present site of Davenport. They met, traded peacefully with Black Hawk at Saukenuk, and, after two days, launched their boats again. But this time the British brought word that Ft. Shelby had fallen and urged the Indians to attack. They did, eagerly, a short ways upstream at what is now Credit Island. One of the boats was sunk, and many soldiers were killed or wounded before the rest managed to escape down river.

With the aid of Sauk, Mesquakie, and Winnebago, the British managed to control the Upper Mississippi Valley until the war was over in 1814.

It took the Americans only a short time before they came back with strength. In 1814, a future president, Zachery Taylor, and 334 soldiers attacked Credit Island near the present day site of Davenport. They encountered 50 British, who had been alerted of the attack, and 1,000 Indians. The battle lasted for several hours. During a lull in the battle, the badly

63

CAMBELL'S ISLAND
CREDIT ISLAND

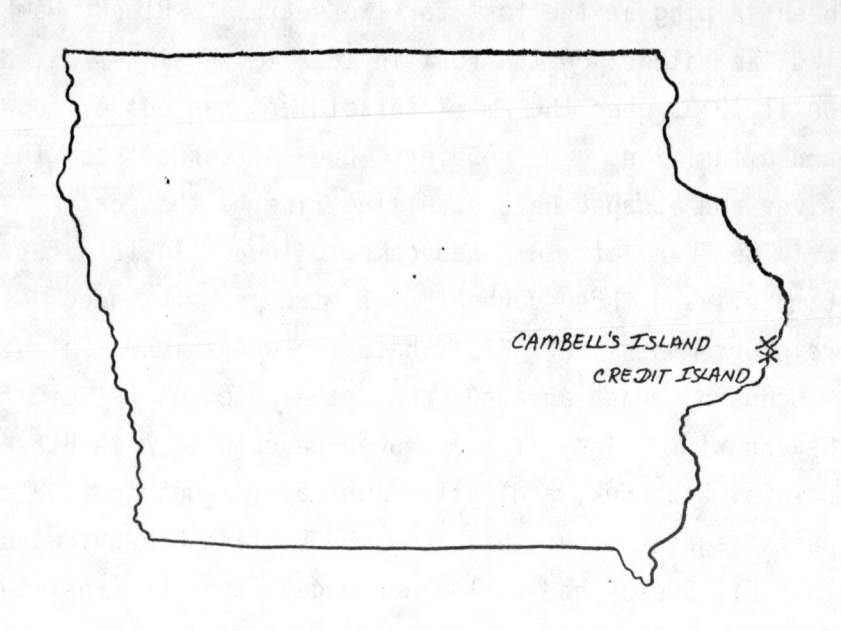

outnumbered and outgunned Americans managed to burn the Sauk and Mesquakie villages and escape downriver. This battle left the British in command of the Upper Mississippi for the remainder of the war.

Even though the Americans met with little success in the Mississippi River Valley, they won the war and forced the British to leave the Iowa country and permanently return to Canada. The Indians were forced to pay for the destroyed property or not to be paid for the lands they deeded over in 1804. This added more insult and frustration twenty years later when the Indians were forced to vacate the lands they neither wanted to leave, nor were to be paid for.

In 1812, the Iowa country became part of the Missouri territory. The first government officials had finally arrived in St. Louis. After the war with Britain, the United States government built Ft. Armstrong on Rock Island, opposite future Davenport. It was a better site than the ruined Ft. Madison. With Fort Armstrong came traders and settlers.

OLD FORT ARMSTRONG, ON ROCK ISLAND

On the Missouri River, things were also happening. In 1819, Major Long with the steamboat "Western Engineer" was making his way up the Missouri from St. Louis. Major Long was sent to explore the river, map out sites for trading posts and search for settlements. He camped in Kainsville, later named Council Bluffs, where Lewis and Clark had also camped fifteen years before. This trip opened the western part of the area to travelers and a few hearty trappers and traders. Major Long later returned to Kainsville via horseback. He was the first explorer to enter the southwest part of the state. He gave reports of finding great seas of grasses and many campfires.

Major Long's Route

× COUNCIL BLUFFS
IOWA
MISSOURI
MISSOURI RIVER
ILLINOIS
ST. LOUIS ×

The next year, 1820, Major Steven Kearny and 21 soldiers journeyed across the state to the Mississippi via what is now Emmetsburg and Northwood. This was the first of 3 journeys he was to make in Iowa. Kearny did the most thorough exploring of any military man or civilian.

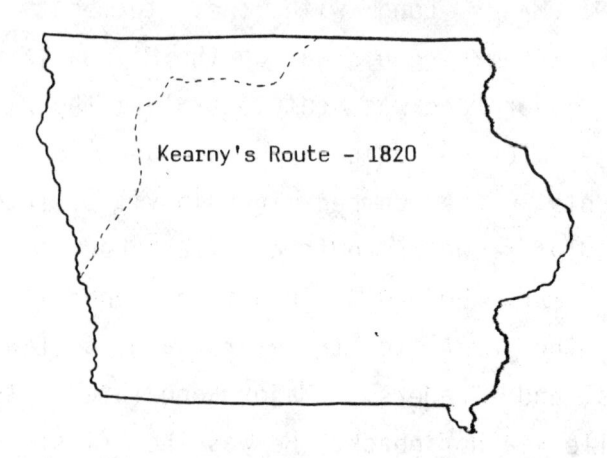

Kearny's Route - 1820

The life of an exploring mounted soldier was not an easy and carefree campout. There were long rides each day through an unknown land with no roads or landmarks. Food was often scarce. Summer brought heat and drenching rain. Winter barracks were cold and drafty. Sometimes the mosquitoes were so thick that the soldiers on horseback were forced to wear nets to escape the insect attacks.

Kearny reported that although the country was beautiful, it would never support more than a thinly scattered population. The belief held by many frontiersmen at the time was that if the land had no trees, it was supposed to be very, very bad farmland. Later, Iowa farmers found the opposite to be true.

In 1821, Missouri became a state and for the next thirteen years, the Iowa country had no government. During this time however, civilization, with all of its ills and blessings, was creeping ever closer. Halfbreeds, the children of red and white parents, were rejected by both groups. In 1824, a special tract of land was given by the Sauk and Mesquakie as a place for the children of these marriages to live.

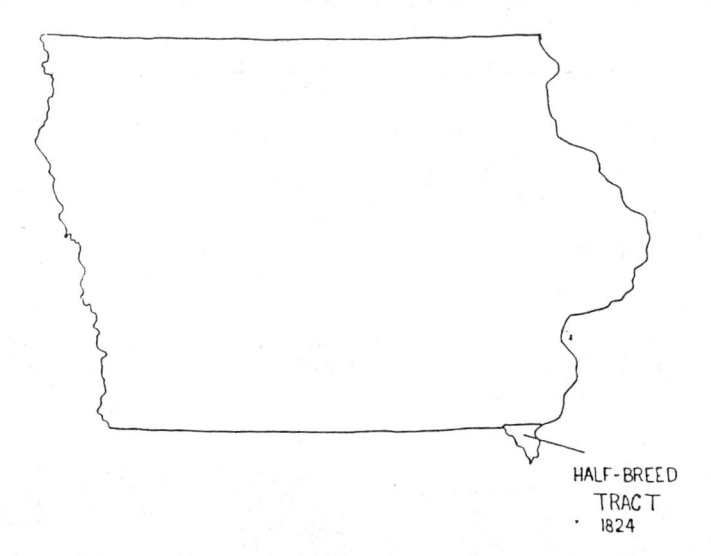

HALF-BREED
TRACT
1824

It formed a triangle bounded by the Des Moines and Mississippi Rivers and was called the halfbreed tract. Unfortunately, the region was noted for its lawlessness in the 10 years of its existence. After the congress allowed the mixed blood people to acquire title to these lands in 1834, most of it fell into the hands of whites.

Iowa was wilderness, and the various tribes still had trouble getting along. The biggest problems existed between two groups, the allied Sauk and Mesquakie tribes, and the Sioux. This feuding probably made it much easier for the whites to succeed in taking over the land later. The Indians asked or were told to ask that the whites settle the problem. It was decided in 1830 that both the Sauk and Sioux give up a strip twenty miles wide and 200 miles long on Iowa soil. Neither tribe was to enter it. This plan didn't work very well and the Winnebagoes, whom the government wanted to move from Wisconsin territory,

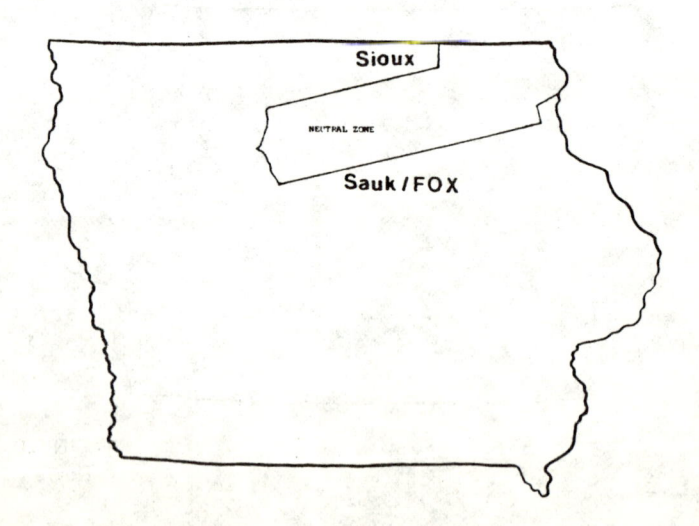

Ft. Atkinson

were brought in much later to serve as a buffer between the two hostile nations. To insure the peace, Ft. Atkinson was built in 1840. The strip was called the neutral ground. The idea of a neutral area was an experiment, but it was a bad one for 1830. There were no boundary lines and tribes were now confined to smaller hunting grounds, so neither side stopped wandering into the area and many fights still broke out between the Sioux and the Sauk and Mesquakie. The unfortunate Winnebagoes, who didn't want to be there in the first place, were stuck in the middle.

In the midst of this problem, two soon-to-be famous men were also in Iowa. Robert E. Lee, later the top Confederate general, was surveying in the southeast. Jefferson Davis, the future president of the Confederacy, was building a sawmill on the Yellow River.

1832 was a red-letter year for the future course of Iowa. Henry Schoolcraft and John Nicolas Nicollet both mapped the area, and their glowing reports of its treasure aroused much interest among the settlers who had moved into Illinois and the surrounding states.

One of the first maps of Iowa.

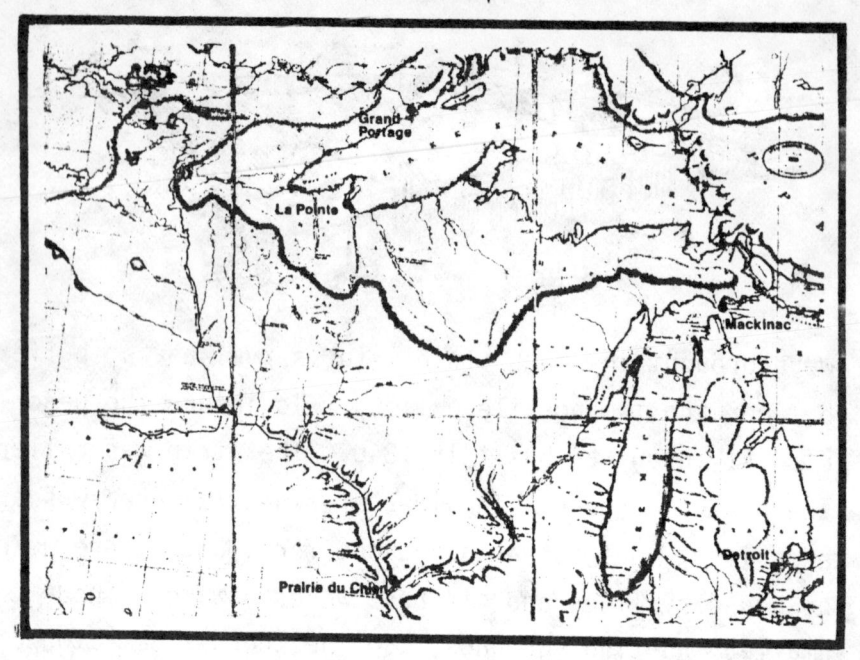

Some equally notable private individuals left equally vivid reports of the Iowa country. An Italian adventurer G.C. Beltrami, journeyed up the Mississippi in 1823 aboard the "Virginia" and chronicled the first steamboat voyage along the eastern border of Iowa. Caleb Atwater left a similar account of his trip as far as Prairie du Chien aboard the "Red Rover" in 1829. During the 1830's, the famous American artist - George Catlin - recorded with brush and pen the daily life of the Indians' dwelling in Iowa land. Two famous English authors - Charles Augustus Murray and Captain Fredrick Marryat - penned interesting accounts of the eastern part of the state in the mid-thirties. These people did much to generate interest in and make people want to come to Iowa.

(Courtesy State Historical Society of Iowa)

The Steamboat "Black Hawk"

The western lands and westward movement had become very important. These two themes had been a major influence in electing Andrew Jackson who was born and raised on the frontier. He had won the election because of his reputation as an Indian fighter. He pursued a policy of moving the Indians in the east to the west of the Mississippi. This removal was to be accomplished by 1840. The settling of the Mississippi Valley became very important to the people of the United States.

Remember, Indians still occupied the Iowa country, and the only other people there were there only by permission of the United States government. However, in 1831, illegal settlers in Illinois occupied Saukenuk, the Sauk's main village. The United States and its settlers occupied lands by a policy they called Manifest Destiny. This meant that it was their right to claim and settle as much land as they needed.

71

Manifest Destiny

    Black Hawk remembered, but still did not accept the 1804 treaty that gave the Illinois land to the whites. At that time, the Illinois militia moved the Indians, who had been mistreated by the settlers for 3 years, to Iowa. In 1832, Black Hawk held a pow-wow with Neapope, a Sauk brave who had gone to Canada to ask the British for help to recover the lands.

    Neapope said that the British would come down from Canada to help if Black Hawk would take the warpath. He also promised the help of the Winnebagoes. This was enough to convince the chief to act. The "war" that was to follow led to the loss of all the Indian lands in Iowa.

    The first week in April, 1832, Black Hawk and his band crossed the Mississippi River. This was the start of the Black Hawk War. From there he headed

(Courtesy State Historical Society of Iowa)
(From a Lithograph Copy of a Painting by C. B. King)
Black Hawk

north along the Rock River in Illinois. His plan was to join the Winnebagoes near Prophet's town and then the combined force would meet the British in Wisconsin.

Throughout 1832, the United States government formed militia units throughout Illinois and Wisconsin. The most famous of these enlisted leaders was Abraham Lincoln, who was to become an Iowa landowner because of his service in the war.

It soon became clear to the Indians that the British were not coming. Upon hearing this, the Winnebagoes became neutral. As the war progressed, they and the Sioux openly helped the Americans. By the time he reached southern Wisconsin even Black Hawk knew he would receive no help. The Sauk chief was able to cause some problems, but the war was really only a series of short skirmishes.

73

Map of Black Hawk War.

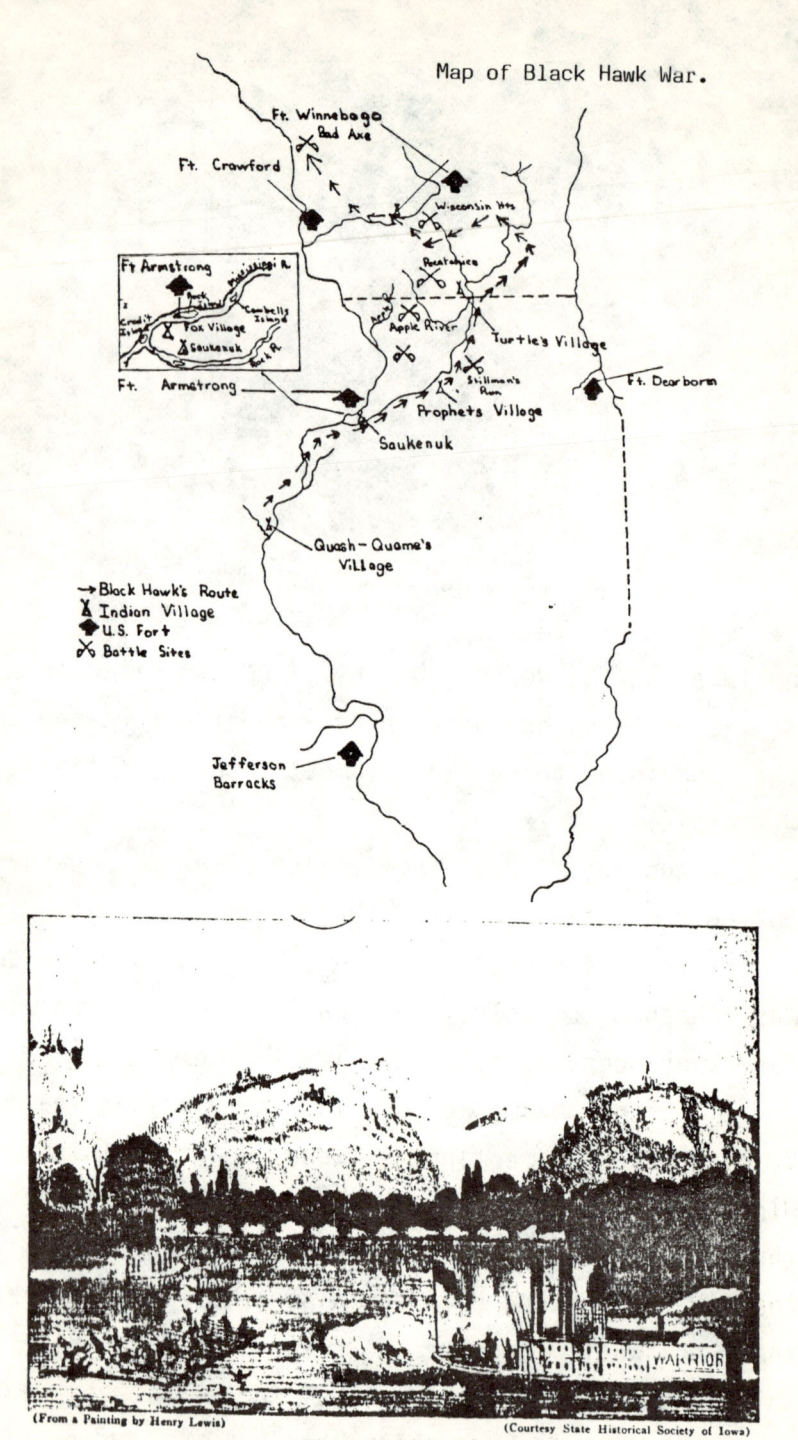

(From a Painting by Henry Lewis) (Courtesy State Historical Society of Iowa)

The Battle of Bad Axe

As the fortunes of the band worsened, many Indian volunteers slipped away and returned to their own bands. The final defeat came at the Bad Axe River where the tribe was forced into the river only to be picked off by the Sioux and an American cannon on a steamboat. Black Hawk escaped, but his hiding place was revealed by the turncoat Winnebagoes. He was sent in irons to Jefferson Barracks in St. Louis, Missouri.

All the Indians of the region paid the price for the war. For instance, the Mesquakies were forced to sell land because of the war even though they had not been involved in any of the fighting. In fact, the Sauks and Mesquakies, who were at times allies, were growing farther and farther apart since 1800. The U S. government, however, insisted on treating the two tribes as one.

General Winfield Scott presided at the peace conference. The treaty signing was at Ft Armstrong in 1832. Keokuk was made spokesman for all the tribesmen and was given 400 square miles as a reward for not taking part in the war. The remainder of the Sauk and Mesquakie were given cash, tobacco and salt. For this payment, they were to withdraw from a strip of land 50 miles wide along the west bank of the Mississippi. This included Dubuque, Delaware, Jackson, Jones, Clinton, Scott, Muscatine, Des Moines, Henry, Lee and parts of eight other present day counties.

The Indians agreed to leave by June 1, 1833. The whites had acquired the land by the usual method

Courtesy Iowa State Department of History and Archives
LE CLAIRE AND THE INDIANS

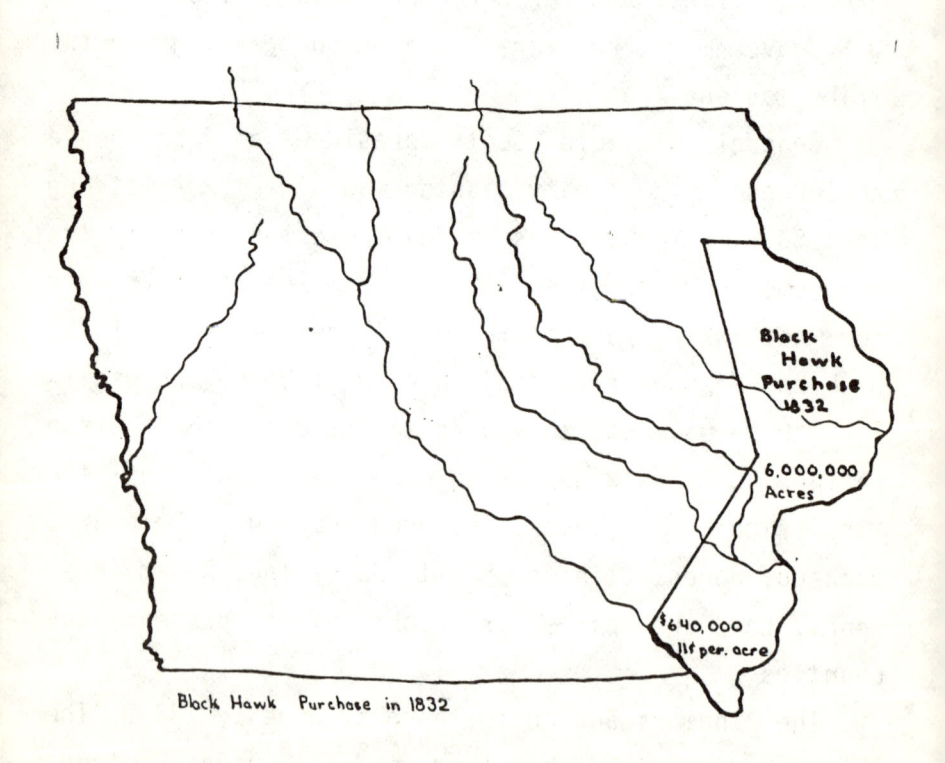

Black Hawk Purchase 1832
6,000,000 Acres
$640,000
11¢ per acre

Black Hawk Purchase in 1832

76

This method had been outlined by Thomas Jefferson. This was described in a previous chapter The war itself was one more conflict between two cultures. The same struggles had been going on since the first tribal family was pushed out by a stronger and more advanced group about 12,000 years ago.   These struggles continued right up until the time the Sauk pushed out the Ioway, and in turn, the white pushed out the Sauk.

So we saw in this chapter that the Americans were slowly paving the way for permanent legal settlement. After they eliminated the threat from foreign powers such as England, scouted the territory, won the Black Hawk War, and provided the policy of cession, they were finally able to legally settle the land they had bought from France in 1804.

CHAPTER VI

We learned in the last chapter that the Americans were moving toward settlement on land west of the Mississippi River--land in present day Iowa. These early Americans explored the land and drove the British out. They finally acquired the foothold they needed to the land, which they insisted the defeated Sauk and Fox Indians sell to them. The United States government purchased that portion of Iowa from the Indian tribes in the treaty of 1832. The land Ordinance of 1785 provides for the land to be surveyed and sold before it could be claimed and settled. The acquired land was governed by the Ordinance of 1785.

No white man could even claim squatter's rights or live on the land until the Indians were legally removed on June 1, 1833. These men were called squatters because they literally sat on the land waiting until they could buy it. Once they legally bought the land, they could be called settlers.

However, squatters had to be forcibly evicted and burned out by the military which made frequent trips through the territory for this purpose. Jefferson Davis, future president of the Confederacy, burned out 12-15 families at Burlington and Ft. Madison. Some squatters were missed because their cabins were located far off the beaten path. One of these was Peter Williams near Ft. Madison who was burned out twice before he finally hid the cabin well enough to avoid detection.

The military's practice of keeping whites out was very odd, because the year before the same troops were protecting the settlers from the Indians. The entire area was not cleared of Indians until 1836.

After June 1, 1833, settlers poured onto the land as fast as they could although they could not legally buy it until 1838. Scores of white families lined up before daylight and crossed the river on three hastily

79

built ferries. The ferries were located at Dubuque, Burlington and Rockingham (near Davenport). Some settlers didn't wait even for the boats, but ferried themselves over by swimming their horses. In one month as many as 1743 wagons bound for Iowa passed through Peoria, Illinois.

Once a settler reached Iowa, he staked a claim to a piece of land. A claim was staked by stepping off the distances. Fifteen hundred paces was accepted as being 320 acres. Stakes were put at the 4 corners or trees marking the corners were blazed (notched or cut). The measurements weren't accurate but the surveyors would straighten out the differences later.

In order to protect a claim for 6 months, a settler usually had to plow up at least 5 acres of

Example of a claim that had been staked.

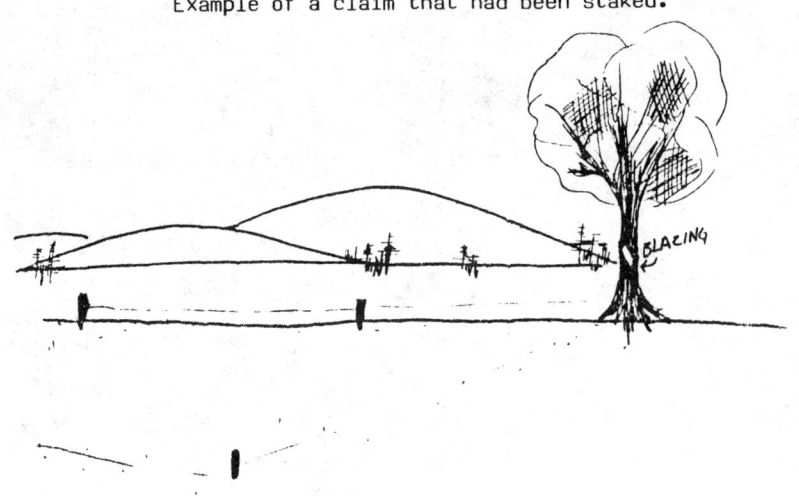

sod. If he built a cabin "eight logs high with a roof," it was safe for an additional 6 months and enabled the "owner" to be a part of and secure the protection of a claim club of his neighbors.

In 1830 about 300 non-Indian people lived in the Iowa country. By 1834, the population was about 5,000. Even though these newcomers built homes and farmed the land they still didn't own any of it. It had yet to be surveyed before it could be sold.

There was always the danger that someone else might try to claim that same land or try to out-bid the settler when it came time to buy. To protect themselves against the two possibilities, some settlers formed claims clubs. These were groups of settlers who acted to both protect each other from lawlessness and prevent newcomers from attempting to push any member off the land.

Claims Club

Settler

There were many reasons for this migration westward. European immigrants were forced to go beyond the areas that had already been claimed and settled. Both East and South were thought to be already "crowded" with people. Younger members of

Clearing the land for farming.

large families often chose to move west into new territory where land could be purchased at a low price. Today with all good free land taken up, it's difficult for us to appreciate the great lure Iowa held.

The deep, rich black soil of Iowa was far superior to the thin and stony covering of the east. This soil attracted experienced farmers who were tired of detouring around huge rocks, making their plows blunt on smaller ones and constantly hauling away medium sized ones.

The settlers simply found an unclaimed portion of land, built shelter and proceded to clear the ground for farming. Most of those settlers who came first had only farming in mind. However, very few crops were put in the first year because the settlers arrived late in the season and the prairie sod required great effort to break--usually a 6 to 12 ox

83

"Breaking" the sod

hitch and a special plow. During the first winter, usually the men remained to guard the claim. Most women and children returned to stay with friends or relatives. The 1833-34 winter was exceptionally hard and in Dubuque many people died of cholera.

Many of the settlers came by water routes. Immigrants from Ohio, Pennsylvania, and New York traveled to Pittsburg where they boarded steamboats to travel down the Ohio River to the Mississippi. Steamers moving up the Father of Waters to Iowa completed the trip. Some settlers came up the Mississippi from New Orleans. A third water route was by way of the Great Lakes to Green Bay, Chicago or Milwaukee. From Green Bay settlers could continue westward by way of the Fox and Wisconsin rivers. From Chicago to the Illinois River was another water route.

Other settlers elected to come overland. The settlers streamed across the country in ox carts, on foot and with heavily laden canvas-covered wagons. The Cumberland Road across Ohio, Indiana and Illinois

Map of routes taken by settlers.

was the most favored route. Another road crossed over land from Peoria, Illinois. The numbers traveling on these roads in 1836 and 1837 were described by John B. Newhall when he wrote: "The great thoroughfares of Illinois and Indiana,...would be literally lined with long blue wagons of the emigrants slowly winding their way over the broad prairies--the cattle and hogs, men and dogs and frequently women and children forming the rear of the van--often ten, twenty and thirty wagons in company. Ask them when and where you would, their destination was the Black Hawk Purchase."

The earliest settlers chose land sites close to the rivers. They did this for a variety of reasons. There were no roads, only narrow trails previously used by Indians or fur traders. As a result, rivers were the only highways or routes of travel. A farmer might choose to be near a river because of the abundance of rich soil, trees and irrigation as well as the transportation. In addition, trade centers were located on rivers where goods could be purchased or sold. If a settler wanted to take advantage of this trading he had to be near a river.

Steamboats carried goods and passengers to new towns along the Mississippi.

With steamboats plying the rivers in increasing numbers, the first settlements were set up as trade centers. These early towns also served as places for fuel supplies for steamboats--wood and etc. River towns such as Montrose, Davenport, Burlington, and Buffalo, all provided a center for farmers who wished to sell their products. Other towns such as Keokuk, Clinton, Dubuque, and Ft. Madison were also settled for this reason. Other towns such as Bloomington (Muscatine) prospered as trading posts and wood yards for steamboats.

The settlers brought their old attitudes and customs with them from their previous homes. They

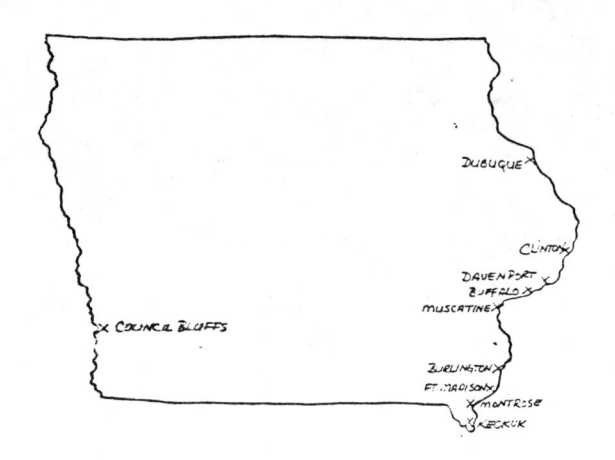

[Map of Iowa with locations marked: Dubuque, Clinton, Davenport, Buffalo, Muscatine, Council Bluffs, Burlington, Ft. Madison, Montrose, Keokuk]

wanted to establish the same way of life they had left in the east and south. With the absence of organized courts and peace officers, claims clubs, and in some cases, miners courts and vigilante groups were formed. Grammar schools and colleges were being built to handle education. The various religious groups erected meeting places to carry on their faith and circuit riding ministers traveled the country and held services for the outlying pioneers.

The U. S. government established forts in the Iowa district and the nearby Indian territory to prevent problems between Indian tribes and between Indians and whites. Although the Indian tribes generally were not a threat to Iowa settlers, the settlers naturally felt uneasy about the closeness of tribal villages. The tribes, squeezed onto smaller living and hunting areas also came in conflict with each other more easily than in the past. This caused them more trouble.

In 1834, Colonel Stephen Kearny arrived in the Iowa District with three companies of dragoons, or

KEARNEY'S ROUTE - 1835

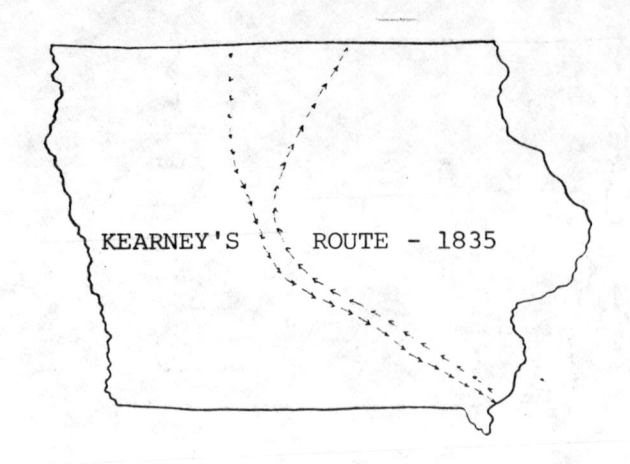

mounted soldiers. They built Ft. Des Moines in 1834 at Montrose where they spent a miserable winter. When spring came, they marched through the western lands to show the Indians the military power that was ready to protect the new settlers. More important, Kearny also scouted the area and prepared a map. He was amazed at the lack of trees, as were the early explorers. They encountered increasingly taller and taller prairie grasses. The Americans had been raised in very wooded areas east of the Mississippi and didn't know quite what to make of the great central prairies of Illinois and beyond eastern Iowa. His route took him from Montrose on the Mississippi River, up the Des Moines River and north to Minnesota. This three month trip covered north central, central, and southeast portions of Iowa, about 800 miles. The journey provided complete and valuable information about portions of the territory that had not been explored and established the site for a second Fort Des Moines--now the present-day capital. Dragoons kept order on the

Dragoon

unsettled frontier until about 1847.

In 1834 the Iowa District became part of the Michigan Territory. The Iowa land had not been part of any territory since 1821. This lack of official law or leadership hadn't meant much as there was very little need for either since there were very few whites and the Indians had their own tribal laws and leaders.

Once Iowa became part of the Michigan Territory, the territorial governor, Mr. Mason, established counties and a government. This act also gave the white settlers representation in the government. Mason created the two large counties of Dubuque and Des Moines. Later they were divided into the smaller counties that we now know.

In 1836, Michigan was ready to become a state, and Iowa became part of the territory of Wisconsin. Henry Dodge was appointed governor and located the capitol at Belmont, Wisconsin. There were now about 10,500 people in the Iowa District. The population had

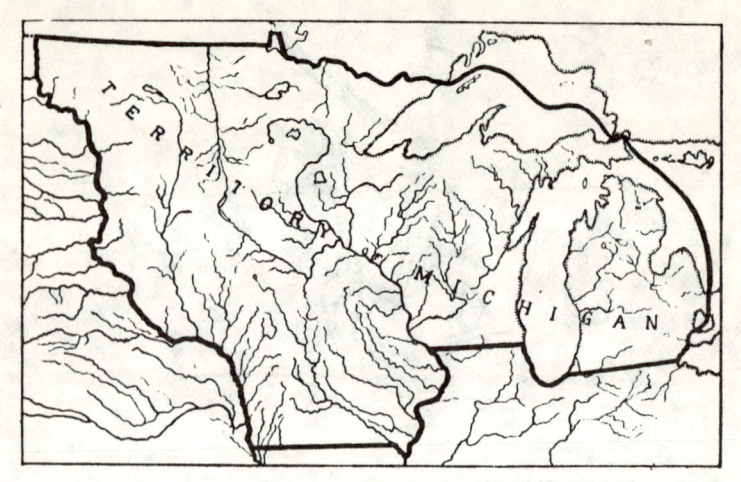

Michigan Territory (Courtesy State Historical Society of Iowa)

Map of Territory of Wisconsin (Courtesy State Historical Society of Iowa)

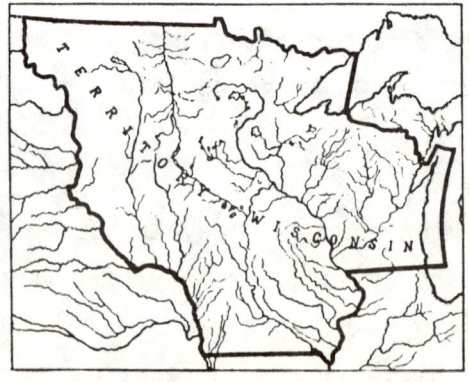

First Territorial Capitol

doubled in two years. The large county of De Moine had been divided into 21 smaller counties.

The new capitol city at Belmont provided few necessities and ever fewer comforts. So the legislators looked for a better site in which to hold their sessions. The city of Burlington offered to build a building at no cost to the legislature if the capitol was moved there. So in 1837, the site was moved, and settlers west of the Mississippi River had a government located close by. The building burned, however, so the legislators met in storerooms. The next two sessions in 1838 were held in the brick Methodist Church, later called "Old Zion".

At this same time a fort was built in the western part of the state at what was later called Council Bluffs. The friendly Pottawattamie Indians requested the fort for protection from the Sioux. This part of the territory was still owned by the Indians.

BLOCKHOUSE AT COUNCIL BLUFFS
Erected in 1838

In the eastern end of the state, in 1836 and 1837, the beaten Sauk and Fox sold an additional 1,250,000 acres west of the original purchase to pay their debts. They agreed to sell for 20 cents an acre. In 1842, the Sauk and Mesquakie agreed to give up the rest of their land in central and western Iowa. This sale caused the final ruination of the tribes, already defeated by the white military and their diseases.

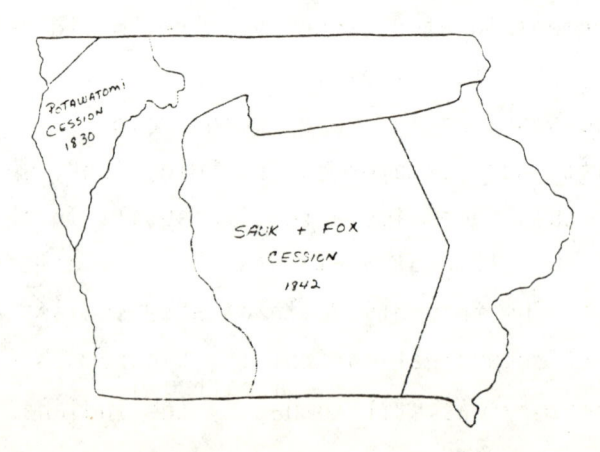

POTAWATOMI CESSION 1830

SAUK + FOX CESSION 1842

YEAR	APPROXIMATE POPULATION
1830	300
1834	5,000
1836	10,500
1838	23,000

The division and settling of this land would follow the same plan as the earlier Indian lands.

As more and more people moved into the Black Hawk Purchase, the desire to have even more land increased. The government concluded two more treaties with the Sauk and Mesquakie, one for Keokuk's Reserve and the other, called the Second Purchase.

Within the space of five years, the settlers had moved onto one-third of the present state of Iowa. The population had grown from 300 in 1830, to almost 23,000 in 1838. Schools, settlements, transportation, religion and some law had appeared. The next step was an orderly approach to statehood.

93

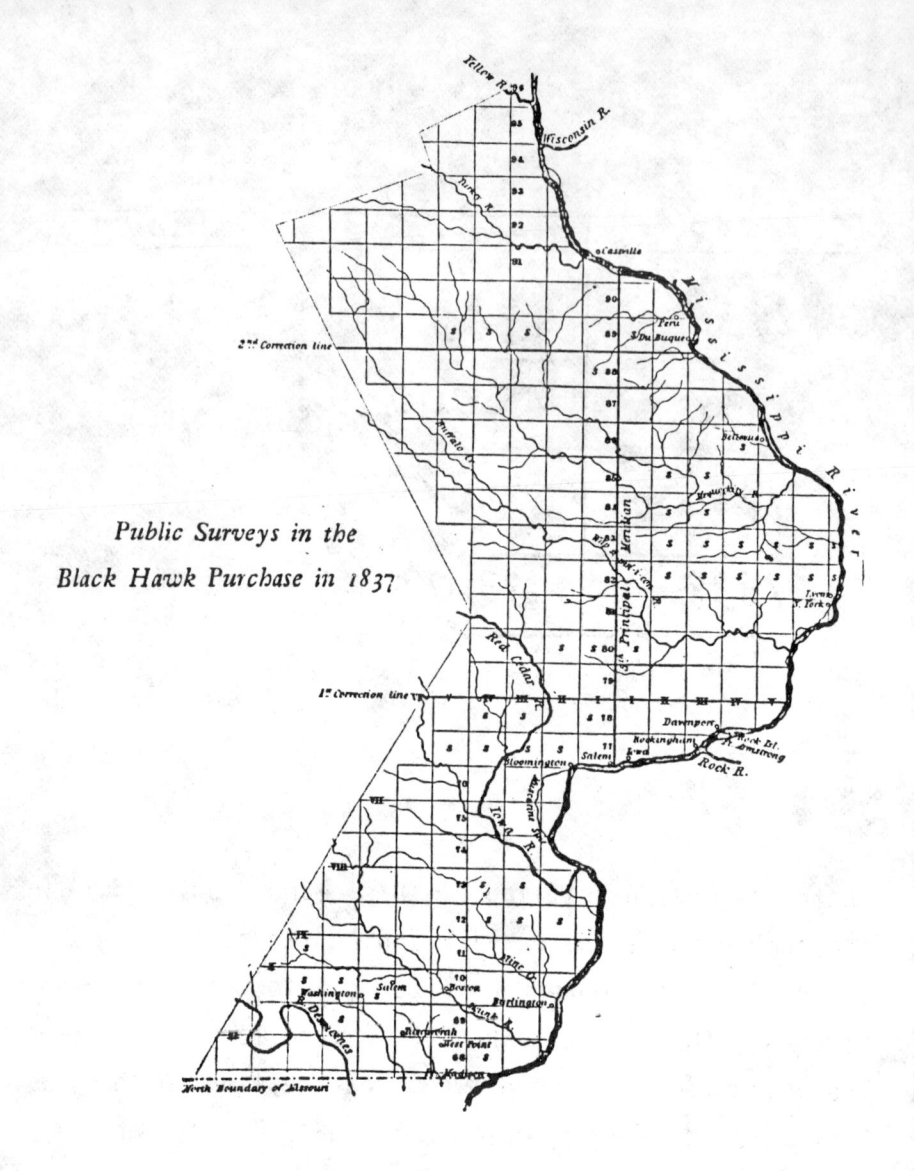

Public Surveys in the Black Hawk Purchase in 1837

CHAPTER VII

We saw in the last chapter that in five years, from 1833 to 1838, the United States acquired almost one-third of the present state of Iowa through treaties with the Indians. The population increased from 300 in 1830 to almost 23,000 by 1838. Schools, settlements, transportation, churches and some law had appeared. However, much more was in store for Iowa before it was to become a state.

At the time that the United States Congress created the Wisconsin Territory in 1836, there were people planning for an Iowa Territory. There was good reason for this. The Wisconsin territory contained the present states of Wisconsin and Iowa, most of Minnesota and parts of North and South Dakota. Plans to move the territorial capital from Burlington to Madison were under way. This would put the territorial government a long distance from the people in the Iowa District. Elected representatives would have to travel over one hundred miles to attend the territorial legislature meetings. Criminal trials and other court cases might be delayed for months before a judge traveled to the district.

The Wisconsin Territorial Legislature met and wrote a request for a separate territory to be established west of the Mississippi River. The request went to the United States Congress. The legislature also asked Congress to help solve the dispute over the Missouri-Iowa boundary location.

Congress agreed that there should be a new Territory of Iowa. President Martin Van Buren signed the bill that created the territory. Because the date for the creation of the territory was July fourth, Iowa residents celebrated both events in 1838. Boundaries for the new territory included the Missouri River on the west, the Mississippi River on the east,

Map of Territory of Iowa (Courtesy State Historical Society of Iowa)

the state of Missouri on the south and Canada on the north.

President Van Buren appointed Robert Lucas to the three year term of territorial governor. Robert Lucas had grown up in Virginia and moved to Ohio as a young surveyor when that state was a part of the western frontier. Lucas settled in Ohio, and at the time that the United States government was concluding its first treaties to purchase land in Iowa, Lucas became Ohio's governor. In 1838, the president asked him to move to a new frontier, the one in Iowa. Lucas accepted this new responsibility and moved from his comfortable home in Ohio to the Iowa territory.

One of the first things Lucas needed to do when he arrived was to choose a site for the territorial capital. Before doing this, he toured the cities and towns located along the shores of the Mississippi River. In this way, Lucas became acquainted with the

Courtesy, State Historical Society
ROBERT LUCAS

area he was to govern. He also could make an informed decision about the location for the capital. He selected Burlington.

Lucas guided the territorial legislature toward planning a responsible government. Even when he knew his advice would be unpopular, he refused to allow unnecessary spending by the legislators. Many times legislators sharply disagreed with Lucas, but he stood firm. This strength helped Iowa when in 1839 the state of Missouri tried to claim a strip of land along the Iowa and Missouri border. The exact location of the boundary was unclear because of a mistake in one of the early surveys. When Missouri officials tried to collect taxes from people who believed they were really living in Iowa trouble began. Both Iowa and Missouri sent soldiers to the area. Lucas called for a decision by the federal government. After the land was resurveyed and the history of the boundary was gathered, the Supreme Court settled the argument. In all, it took twelve years to solve the problem.

Burlington was to serve only as a temporary capital, so in his first speech to the legislature Robert Lucas suggested that a committee of three choose a place further west for the territorial capital. Several towns hoped to be selected. The citizens of Mount Pleasant believed their city was just the place. Residents of almost thirty towns also hoped their towns would be chosen. Finally, three men were sent to Johnson County to find a new unsettled site for the seat of government, to be called Iowa City.

Capitol at Iowa City

The three representatives found a good place on the Iowa River. It had a good landing site for steamboats and flatboats which would bring both people and needed supplies to the capital city. "The site of the location is of unrivalled beauty allowing the eye to stretch for a great distance over a handsome prairie." wrote John B. Newhall.

By 1838, the Iowa population had reached 23,242. Yet, there had not yet been a government land sale so that people could buy the land they already lived on. Finally, in November of that year, the government began the land sales for which the farmers, business people, townspeople and homebuilders had waited so long. The government sold land for $1.25 per acre. Cash, gold or silver, was required. The government did not accept paper money because it was sometimes worthless.

Sometimes settlers did not have enough money to purchase the land they wanted. When this happened, a settler could find a land speculator at the sale who was willing to purchase the land and then re-sell it to a settler. In this way, the settler could pay for the land over a number of months, paying interest to the speculator. Speculators earned money, and the farmers got the land they wanted.

There were several reasons why people decided to move to Iowa. The fine agricultural land attracted many in a time when farming was the nation's major occupation. Settlers also felt safe moving to the Iowa country because the Indian tribes had been removed from the area. There were good transportation routes to the Iowa country. Letters from settlers reached the east, encouraging friends and relatives to migrate to the territory. Guidebooks described the territory in words that were sure to attract newcomers. Newspapers, too, carried stories about the richness and beauty of the area, attracting settlers.

Steamboats, stagecoaches, and wagons provided transportation for those traveling to Iowa. People in eastern states traveled down the Ohio River and then up the Mississippi. Those coming from the southern states boarded boats headed up the Mississippi River from New Orleans or Memphis. By 1840, four hundred steamboats churned through the waters of the Ohio and Mississippi Rivers. The boats traveled about seven miles per hour. To save money, a passenger could travel on the deck instead of a cabin. Some passengers paid part of their fare by chopping wood for the boat's furnace. Travel by steamboat did have risks. Sometimes boats ran aground, steam boilers exploded, or fires broke out.

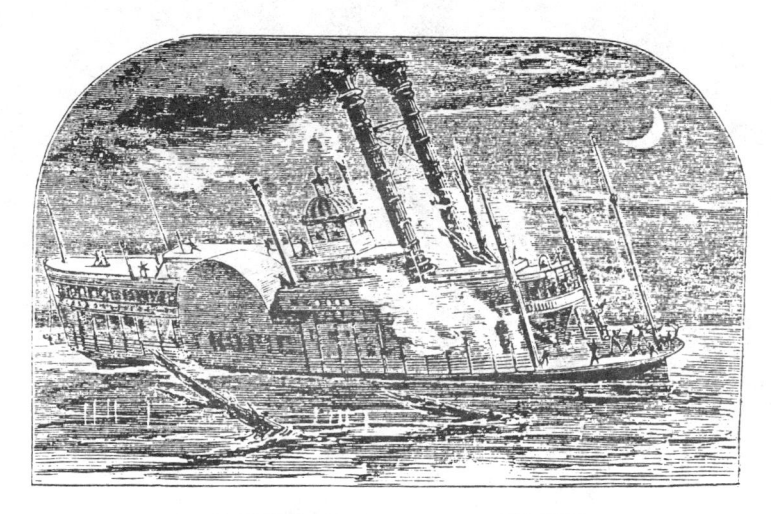

A MISSOURI RIVER STEAMER SNAGGED

When travelers arrived at their riverport destination, they continued their journey overland on foot, by wagon, or stagecoach. When the first settlers arrived in Iowa country there were no roads for them to use. But here and there trails had been worn in the earth by Indian feet, or animal hooves.

(Courtesy State Historical Society of Iowa)

Stagecoach About 1850

These trails often became the roads that settlers used. Of course these roads were not paved, and rain created a muddy impassible quagmire. There were no bridges across streams. Travelers either found a shallow place to ford the stream, or cut trees to make a bridge. At busy crossings, someone usually started a ferry business, charging a fee for taking people, animals, and wagons across.

Because roads were so important for travel, the first territorial legislature created many laws about roads, ferries, and bridges. These laws were meant to improve travel conditions.

Some newcomers traveled to Iowa by stagecoach. There were connections from the east as far as the Mississippi River. In the early territorial years, there were few stagecoaches for travelers because there were not enough people or freight to make the stagecoach business profitable. Stagecoach transportation within the territory was quite limited. Stagecoaches first came to Iowa to carry mail to and

> ## Stage Office,
>
> On Iowa Avenue, between Clinton and Dubuque Streets.
>
> STAGES LEAVE FOR THE
>
> *West*—For Ft. Des Moines and Council Bluffs, at 7 o'clock, A.M. and 1 o'clock P.M.
> *North*—For Cedar Rapids and Dubuque, at 7 o'clock, A.M.
> *Northwest*—For Cedar Rapids, Vinton and Waterloo, at 1 P.M.
> *South*—For Washington, Oskaloosa and Fairfield, at 8 o'clock A.M.
>
> OMNIBUSES RUN TO AND FROM THE CARS, carrying passengers either way. Persons in the city wishing to leave on the cars, will leave their address at the Stage Office.
>
> ## Chas. J. Tegde, Agent

from the territory. When stagecoach connections could be found, newcomers traveling overland used this means of transportation. Once the settlers arrived, they proceeded to locate the land they hoped to farm. The first settlers in Iowa Territory chose forest covered land near the rivers. The logs from the trees could provide material to quickly build a home or shelter If someone had set up a sawmill nearby, lumber might be used instead of logs. Some settlers eventually built homes using nearby stone or even locally made brick. Although forests contained game, nut trees, and wild fruits, the pioneer's daily diet remained much the same. Settlers ate what they could grow, gather, hunt, or fish. Corn became a mainstay, and clever frontierswomen created many different ways to serve the grain.

In October, 1842, the government made a final treaty with the Sauk and Mesquakie for their remaining Iowa land. The white settlers had continued to move westward and it seemed impossible to keep the two groups of people separated. The federal government's solution was to purchase more Indian land and once again move the Indians away from the advancing pioneers. This New Purchase opened more land for settlement. The treaty set May first as the date that settlers would be allowed to move on to the land. Word about the chance for new land spread quickly. Weeks ahead of that day in spring, hopeful settlers gathered along the New Purchase boundary. Descriptions published in advance told of beds of coal, beautiful groves, and gently rolling prairies bordering the Des Moines River. Some settlers tried to occupy this land before the first of May. To remove these people and to prevent others from trying to move onto the land a corps of United States dragoons arrived.

While the excited settlers waited for May 1, the former tenants, the Indians, prepared to leave the land they had once been free to hunt and live on.

They soon would leave their beautiful forests and prairies for the dry and barren lands in Kansas.

As April thirty-first ended at midnight, gun shots signaled the hour. People on foot, on horses, and in wagons surged forward to stake the boundaries for their new homesteads or townsites

By 1844 Iowa had become a settled agricultural area with bustling towns and cities There was much talk about statehood. This was the greatest political issue of the time. Governor Lucas' first petition in the legislature in 1839 was to begin the process of statehood that very year. He was so confident that the legislators would accept it that he also suggested the boundaries of the new state. The legislature decided against the proposal, but the boundaries would be an issue later

In 1840 the Iowa territorial legislature had decided to give the citizens a chance to start becoming a state. The first step was to write a constitution, a set of rules that the state would live by. The voters decided not to do this by a vote of 2903 to 937.

In 1842 the proposal to write a constitution was again defeated by a population that had reached 42,000. Those favoring statehood said that as a state, Iowa would attract even more settlers than as a territory. Statehood would also bring the right to have voting representatives in the United States Congress, a true voice in the national government. Voters would also elect their own governor instead of

105

IOWA'S POPULATION

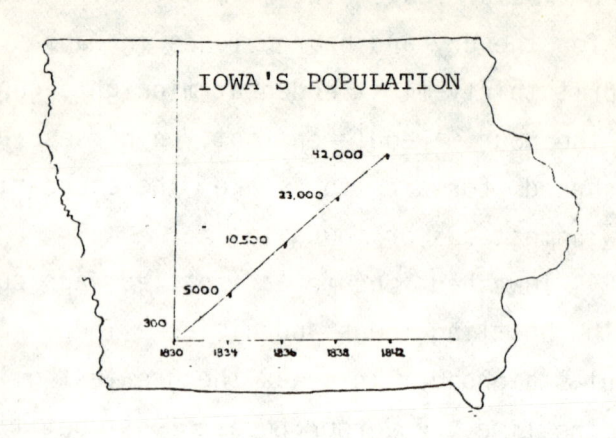

the President appointing one.

Those opposed to statehood believed taxes would become too high, once Iowans had to pay for their own state government. Farmers paying for land didn't want added debts.

Those in favor of statehood finally won. In 1844, the people, pushed by the new governor, John Chambers, voted to write a constitution and request statehood. The territorial legislature wrote a constitution and sent the request along with suggested state boundaries to the United States Congress. The Constitution had taken seventy-two men from 25 counties almost a month to write.

Congress approved the constitution but not the suggested Lucas boundaries. The government agreed to accept Iowa as a state but substituted its own boundaries. These boundaries, suggested by the French explorer, Joseph Nicolett, made a much smaller state. Slavery had become an important issue in the nation. Because of this, northern Congressmen favored small

John Chambers

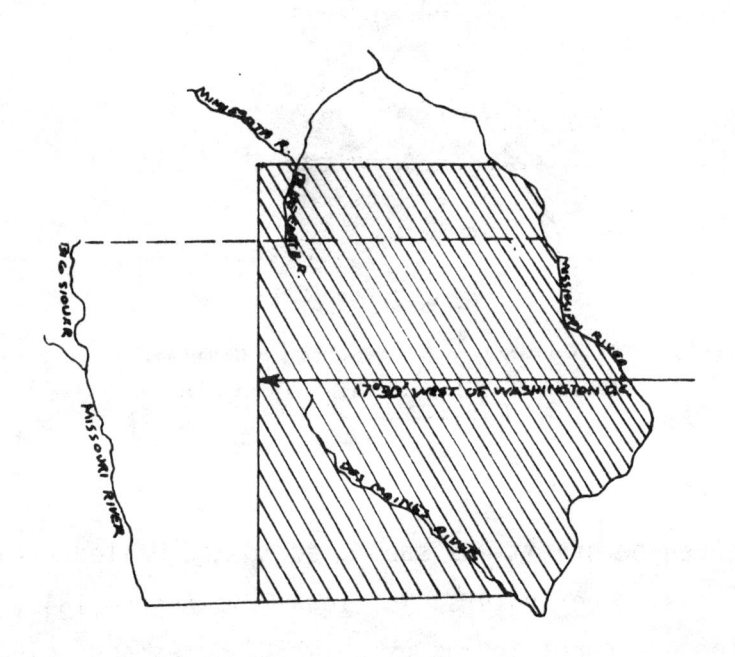

NICOLLET BOUNDARY

states so as to create as many free states as possible from the remaining western lands. Southerners favored large northern states for just the opposite reason.

The people in Iowa rejected Congress' boundary suggestion. This also meant a rejection of statehood. But in 1846 another constitution was written, very much like the one in 1844. With the help of Illinois Representative Stephen A. Douglas, compromise boundaries were decided upon. The constitution went to Congress in December.

Courtesy Iowa State Department of History and Archives
ANSEL BRIGGS, FIRST GOVERNOR
OF THE STATE OF IOWA

Even before it was submitted to the United States Congress, the voters in Iowa, in August 1846, had passed the constitution by only 300 votes and elected and inaugurated a governor--Ansel Briggs, a businessman and stagedriver from Andrew, Iowa. He was governor when there was not yet a state for him to govern.

The Iowans were in a hurry. The reason for this was the slave state-free state issue and the Missouri Compromise of 1820. The Missouri Compromise said that a free state, like Iowa, could only be admitted if a slave state was also admitted into the Union. Florida was ready for statehood. The people who wanted Iowa to become a state didn't want some other northern territory to take Iowa's place. Congress approved the bill for admission and President James K. Polk signed the bill into law on December 28, 1846.

So we saw in this chapter that Iowa was being settled and civilized at a rapid rate. Because of this, it became a territory. After overcoming some boundary and constitutional problems Iowa became a state.

Courtesy Iowa State Department of History and Archives
ANSEL BRIGGS, FIRST GOVERNOR
OF THE STATE OF IOWA

CHAPTER VIII

On that cold day of December 28th, 1846, the first elected governor of Iowa, Ansel Briggs, anxiously awaited word that the Congress of the United States had approved Iowa for statehood. He was told later that Iowa was officially made a state that day. When the news got around, everyone was happy. Many people in the state had been working for a long time to make Iowa a state. The system of government had been started in the spring of that same year. Many important men of the territory met at Burlington in May. Then, meeting at the Zion Methodist Church, they wrote a constitution for the prospective new state. Later in the year, Mr. Briggs was elected governor. Even though there were just over 102,000 white people in the state, those early citizens expected that settlers would soon be flooding the trails that led to and through Iowa. As Indian lands became open for settlement, population grew rapidly. It is said that Wapello County in southeastern Iowa was settled over night following the Sauk and Mesquakie Indian land cession of 1842. Even though many people had immigrated to Iowa already, the largest flood was yet to come.

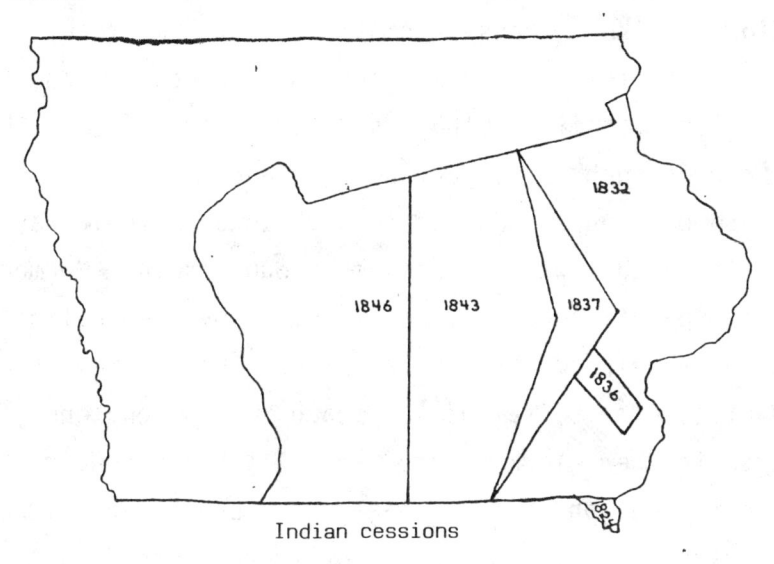

Indian cessions

By 1846, most of the Indians who had lived in the state had given up all claims of ownership of the land. Through a series of treaties and agreements with the U.S. government, tribes sold their rights and were moved out. By 1851, the Sioux were the last tribe to give up their claims to land in Iowa. All that remained were a few small, nomadic bands following the hunting across the state. This was the area that had once been their home, from the

Mississippi on the east to the Missouri on the west.

When the news of low-priced land reached the east, large numbers of settlers headed west for Iowa and other frontier states. Some were there to make their fortunes, to obtain cheap land, to build factories and mills, and to make a better life for themselves and their families. Some came to open mines, evade the law or to improve their health. Iowa's climate was said to be ideal. Most came from older states in the Union, like Pennsylvania, Ohio, New York, and Virginia. There, land was much more expensive and the soil less fertile. Other settlers came from other countries such as Germany and Ireland.

Some groups passed through Iowa on their way to points farther west. One such group was the Mormons, a group of people tied together by deep religious faith. Their search for a place where they could practice their faith in peace was a long one. It began in New York state where their founder and leader, Joseph Smith, began to preach and attract followers. From there, they were forced out of settlements in Ohio and Missouri, finally settling in the 1830's in Nauvoo, Illinois. This was right across the river from the present town of Montrose in southeast Iowa. There, the Mormon town grew rapidly in size and political influence. Soon it was the largest city in Illinois. Many of the non-Mormons feared the Mormons would soon force their beliefs on the entire state. This hatred climaxed when an angry mob gathered at nearby Carthage and murdered Joseph

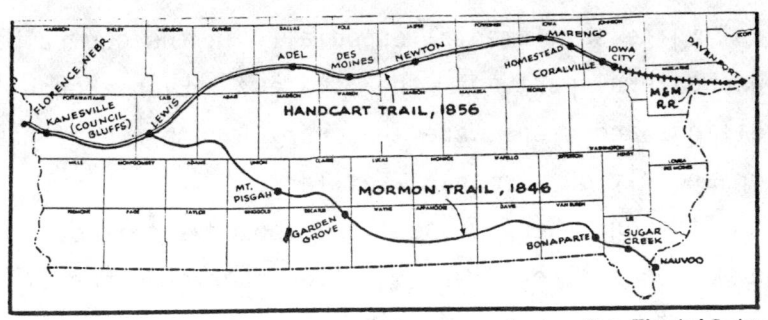

Courtesy, State Historical Society

The Mormon Route Across Iowa.

Smith and his brother.

Threatened by further persecution, the leaders of the church decided to move again. In the late winter of 1846, they crossed over into Iowa on their way to a new homeland in the far west. By summer, there were thousands of Mormons traveling along a route through southern Iowa. Ahead of the main body, went the Brigham Young party who mapped trails, planted crops, and established campsites for those who came after. Campsites were important as they were recommended to other pioneers as places where they could find water and shelter. They are even mentioned in the state immigrant guides of the following years. The trail started in Lee County and continued through Van Buren, Davis, Appanoose, Wayne, Monroe, Lucas, Decatur, Clarke, Union, Adair, Cass and Pottawattamie counties. Many of the sites became towns, such as Farmington, Garden Grove, and Mt. Pisgah. Part of the trail later became what is now part of State Highway 2.

These Mormon camps put thousands of acres of land under cultivation for the first time and were the

113

first white settlements, especially in the central and southwestern part of the state. Even though the dwellings and crops were temporary, both were taken over shortly by permanent settlers.

Although the Iowa settlers looked suspiciously at the Mormon's, there was little outright hostility. The fact that the Mormons were migrating and not settling in an unsettled part of the state gave little opportunity for problems.

While the Saints, as the Mormons called themselves, were camped at Mt. Pisgah in Union county, they were visited by Captain James Allen. Allen was recruiting soldiers. In 1846, the U.S. was at war with Mexico and needed volunteers.

When the Saints realized that they could get to their western destination at government expense, 500 men were directed to enlist. The soldiers' pay was used by the Saints for food and equipment. Other Mormons enlisted as porters, cooks and laundresses.

The journey across the state was very hard because of lack of food, overwork and harsh weather. Death and sickness was a constant companion and almost taken for granted. Burials were made all along the trail. Hundreds of people were buried at Mount Pisgah alone.

Council Bluffs (then known as Kanesville) was the last Iowa stop. The town sprang up almost overnight. Throughout the next 6 years, Mormons from the east continued to flow through Iowa, following the trail and staying at the permanent campsites.

Kanesville, now Council Bluffs, in 1849

Other travelers, also used Iowa as a bridge over which they passed to destinations further west. When gold was discovered in California, people by the thousands went to California in 1849 to search for gold. The same occurred when land opened up in Oregon. Many Iowans got "Oregon Fever". Many more came to stay here, however, and the population of Iowa

YEAR	APPROXIMATE POPULATION
1846	102,000
1850	192,214
1860	674,913

Three covered wagons each labeled "California" crossed the endless prairie.

tripled in those brief years between the 1840 and 1860 census from 102,000 to 650,000.

Long before Iowa became a state, religious missionaries had come to Iowa. But after statehood, many of the churchmen were also educators and townbuilders. Josiah B. Grinnell founded a town that bears his name. Another, Rev. John Todd, came to establish a church and a college. The result was the town and college of Tabor. For many years it was one of the major places for higher education in southwest Iowa.

Although desire for cheap land was the major reason for newcomers to come to the state, some settlers came to Iowa to escape problems at home or to fulfill a dream. Some Germans were fleeing political oppression and military service. For the Irish, it was poverty, made worse by a failure in the potato crop, their main source of food which forced them to seek a new land. Later they came for the chance to work on a railroad. For still others, it was a dream, the hope of establishing a perfect or utopian society, that brought them to the state. Settlements such as the Amanas near Iowa City and the Icarian community, near Corning, are the results of those dreams.

As mentioned before, Iowa's location on the central route to California and points west had a lot to do with people settling here. One of the groups that passed through was a group of 1300 converts to Mormonism on their way to Utah. They had ridden the railroad to Iowa City--the last stop. Because they had very little money, they were forced to pull carts with their belongings from there on. While camped at Coralville, they made 2-wheeled carts. Pushing or pulling their handcarts, they left in four groups. Walking from early morning until late at night, they averaged 25 to 30 miles per day as they trekked through Iowa towards Utah.

Group of Mormons traveling to Utah with their 2-wheeled carts.

Not all the Mormons left Iowa. One group had formed their own settlement under the leadership of Joseph Smith's eldest son. They called themselves the Reorganized Church of Jesus Christ of Latter Day Saints, and used Lamoni as their headquarters. Their high religious standards and educational beliefs added much to the state's culture.

One group that had lived in the state and wanted to return was the Mesquakie Indians. They had been removed to Kansas reservations in 1846, along with the Sauks. By the 1850's, they were totally dissatisfied with the reservation life because of bad water, lack of hunting and disease. In 1856, the tribal leaders decided to buy and live on land in the state they had left. By purchasing and owning land, the Mesquakies were able to preserve their way of life in the heart of white, agricultural Iowa. This is one of the few instances of this happening in the United States, and is the major story of Iowa Indians in the mid and later 1800's.

When the new state joined the union with only 46 of its present 99 counties, most of the population was along the Mississippi on the eastern side of the state. The capitol, Iowa City, was located in the middle of the populated area. It became apparent that a location more in the center of the state would be necessary as the rest of the state became settled. In 1857, the legislature accepted the proposal to move the site of the capitol to Des Moines, at the fork of the Raccoon and Des Moines rivers.

1st capitol at Iowa City.

The search for a location for our state capitol was not an easy one. As early as 1847, the Iowa legislature appointed a commission to select a new site for the Iowa State house to replace Iowa City. The first choice was a place called "Monroe City", now Prairie City, in Jasper County. But there were charges that many of the commissioners owned land near the site, which they did. The legislature turned down their selection.

Many possible sites were then considered. But after several petitions by the residents of Des Moines, it became the choice of the legislature in 1855. Once the town had been chosen, it remained to specify where the capitol building would be located.

119

The legislature appointed another commission to choose such a spot (within 2 miles of the junction of the Raccoon and Des Moines Rivers). The building and the land eventually were to cost the taxpayers of Iowa nothing. Both were to be donated to the state.

First Capitol at Des Moines. November 1857 to July 1886.

In a matter such as this, you must remember that there is a great deal at stake. The location of the capitol would naturally attract people and business to that town. The land near such a site would be worth a great deal of money. Once this is understood, it is easy to understand why competition to have the capitol near their own land caused the citizens of Des Moines, on each side of the river, to go to great lengths to get the capitol on their side. The capitol commissioners considered both sides, then chose to accept a donation of 16 acres of land on the east side. The land is part of what is now the 93-acre capitol complex and grounds.

OUR STATE CAPITOL

To gain the location, the east-siders built a 3-story brick building, which they wanted to donate to the state as the new state capitol. It turned out that the construction costs were paid for with a loan the promoters got from the state school fund, a debt that was later to be cancelled by the legislature despite widespread protest. This building stood at the present location of the Soldiers and Sailors Monument, south of the present statehouse.

Later in 1866, the Dubuque-Herald would sum up the experience as follows: "Many readers will remember how Des Moines became the capitol of the state. The removal of the capitol changed houses into palaces, as far as their value is concerned, and converted men with little money into millionaires."

Such is the story of the relocation of Iowa's Capitol. Not uncommon as such things go, it is a study of speculation and politics, and their influence on the outcome of history.

Despite the state's rapid growth, those first few years were pretty rough, especially for the farmers, which included almost everybody. 1851 saw a gigantic flood because it rained much more than normal. That year it rained 75", twice what it usually does. The rains washed away crops that were the livelihood of the state. In the winter of 1856, there was a blizzard; a great blizzard that isolated and starved both livestock and people. Despite the high claims made for the climate of Iowa in ads of eastern newspapers, it was not quite a Garden of Eden.

Another reason for settlement, in addition to the fertile soil and climate, was the closeness to Chicago, which was rapidly becoming a railroad center for trains from the Atlantic coast states. In addition, Iowa's strategic location for railroads on the way to the Pacific coast brought the young state national attention. The coming of the railroad was one of the most important forces in increasing the population of a state. No factor had greater impact on the states of the West, and until the late 1860's, Iowa was the West.

Railroad construction was discussed in Iowa as early as 1836, when Iowa was a part of the Wisconsin territory. At that time, John Plumbe had proposed that a trans-continental railroad be built from

Courtesy, State Department of History and Archives
An Early Train.

Dubuque west to the Pacific. It was a common concern when citizens decided to write the state's first constitution. While they feared banks and big companies, they welcomed the railroads. Therefore, they did not place railroads under as strict rules.

From the very beginning of statehood, there were many businessmen forming companies to build railroads. Although many were planned, some were never built. Many existed only on paper, never getting past the talking stage. Some men who wanted to build railroads were speculators. Speculators would plan a railroad, get towns to give them money to build it, then leave with the money. This was not uncommon, especially after 1847, when the Iowa legislature passed a law allowing towns and counties to vote to spend tax money to provide transportation. Iowa townspeople lost no time in voting such bonds to bring the railroads to their town. Only the space race of the 1960's can compare to the excitement with which people of the day saw railroads. Most felt that a town without a railroad was a town soon to disappear. In most cases

From an old painting, Courtesy, State Historical Society
Working on the Railroad.

the following years would show just how right that belief was.

Since most railroad lines could follow a number of different routes, townspeople actively competed to be included and the builders actively recruited bond issues. For example, Iowa City raised $50,000 to be paid to the first company to lay rails to the town. That same year, the Central Iowa Railroad folded when promoters left town with the bond money.

The first passenger train in Iowa made the 67 miles from Davenport to Iowa City in January 1856. Later that same year, the U.S. Congress gave railroad promoters the boost they had been asking for. According to a new law, each state would give alternating sections of land on either side of the line to selected railroad companies. The companies could then sell the land and raise funds to construct a railroad. Since a section equals 640 acres, the

124

1st railroad routes

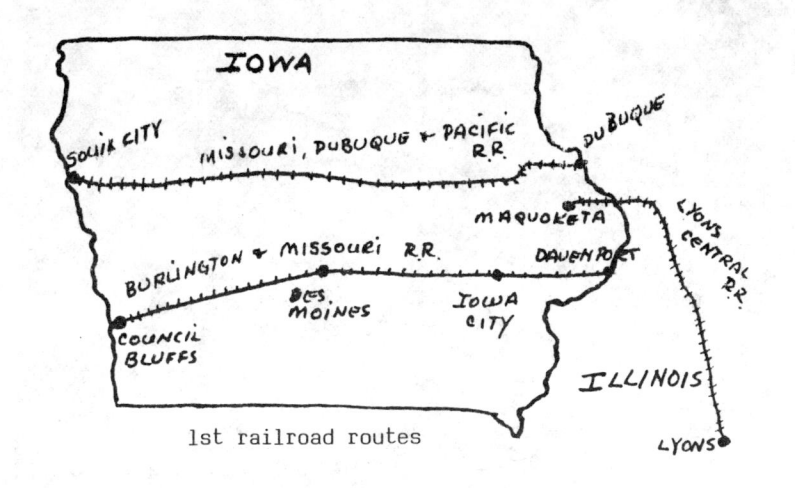

railroads claimed 1/9 of all Iowa land. This is equal to a strip of land 24 miles wide, from the Mississippi to the Missouri. The law further named 5 railroads to cross Iowa from east to west. They were to link up with other railroads, coming from Chicago to towns on the Mississippi, then across the state to Nebraska and South Dakota. They were: the Burlington and Missouri--from Davenport to Council Bluffs by way of Iowa City and Des Moines, the Burlington from Burlington, the Rock Island from Davenport, the Lyons Central or Central Iowa--from Lyons to Maquoketa and the Missouri, and the Dubuque and the Pacific--from Dubuque to Sioux City.

Despite huge amounts of land and money, railroad construction did not increase very fast. The depression of 1857 slowed this building down even more. By the end of 1859, there were still only 500 miles of railroad tracks, operating in Iowa. This was

Mexican War battle

to change very little until after the Civil War.

The importance of Iowa's location to the railroads was just one factor that brought the young state national attention. Another was the fact that Iowa was the first state acquired by the U.S. through the Louisiana Purchase to be admitted to the Union as a "free" state. Iowa began to figure more and more in the slavery issue.

At the time of Iowa's statehood, the U.S. had just acquired much new land as the result of the Mexican War. Even though no soldiers from this state were in the war, many of Iowa's counties are named for heroes and battles of the Mexican War. They include: Buena Vista, Cerro Gordo, Butler, Clay, Fremont, Guthrie, Hardin, Mills, Page, Palo Alto, Ringgold, Scott, Taylor, and Worth.

As the territories formed, they gained population. Soon they began to apply for statehood. Many congressmen were arguing about if and when the territories should be admitted to the Union. Should they be slave states or free states?

The question of slavery became more important with the admission of each new state. In 1854, Senator Stephen A. Douglas of Illinois introduced a bill to organize Nebraska and Kansas as territories. The bill would leave the decision on slavery up to the settlers of each area. To make this possible, it was necessary to repeal the famous Missouri Compromise of 1820, an act many credit with preventing a Civil War. The Douglas Bill passed in May of that same year. Protest meetings were held before and after the passage. One such meeting was held in Crawfordsville, Iowa. This gathering was one of the first of the series which laid the foundations for what became the present day Republican Party. This party soon became closely identified with opposition to slavery. Democrats were seen as divided or opposed to the question.

Some Iowans felt so strongly about slavery, that they were willing to break the law in order to help escaped slaves find freedom. Since Iowa was bordered

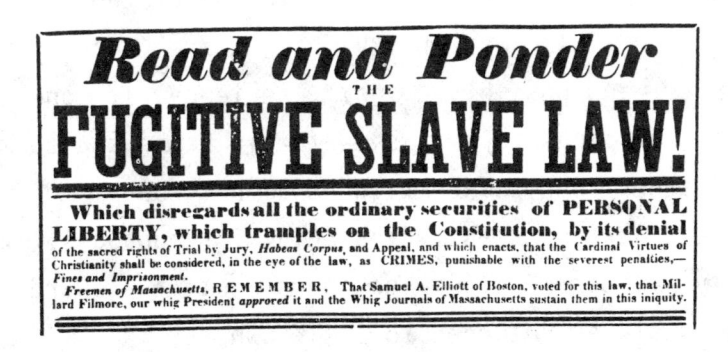

Read and Ponder
THE
FUGITIVE SLAVE LAW!

Which disregards all the ordinary securities of PERSONAL LIBERTY, which tramples on the Constitution, by its denial of the sacred rights of Trial by Jury, *Habeas Corpus*, and Appeal, and which enacts, that the Cardinal Virtues of Christianity shall be considered, in the eye of the law, as CRIMES, punishable with the severest penalties,— *Fines and Imprisonment.*

Freemen of Massachusetts, REMEMBER, That Samuel A. Elliott of Boston, voted for this law, that Millard Filmore, our whig President *approved* it and the Whig Journals of Massachusetts sustain them in this iniquity.

127

by Missouri, a slave state, many blacks seeking freedom crossed over into Iowa. To help them across the state, sympathetic Iowans set up an "underground railroad", an extensive network of hiding places, to aid fugitive slaves escape to Canada. Although it was known as the underground railroad, it really wasn't a railroad, but a series of homes with secret or hidden rooms. The slaves would be moved at night under the cover of darkness, and hidden in a secret room to rest and eat during the daylight hours. The next night they would be moved to the next location or stop, until, hopefully, they would end up in Canada. The stops were about 1 night's drive from each other. If a slave was discovered and captured, it was called a derailment on the underground railroad.

Among the settlers from northern states were people who thought slavery was a great sin. These people were called abolitionists. The new Republican party formed in Iowa agreed. Its members and abolitionists frequently helped runaway slaves. Among the abolitionists, the Quakers were the most outspoken and would go to great lengths to help the escaped slaves. This was risky, as there were fines, lawsuits, and possibly a jail sentence if one was caught helping. Their sympathetic beliefs also made them rather unpopular with the neighbors. Slave catchers were constantly searching for runaways. Like bounty hunters, slave catchers got a reward for runaway slaves returned to their owners.

The Underground Railroad

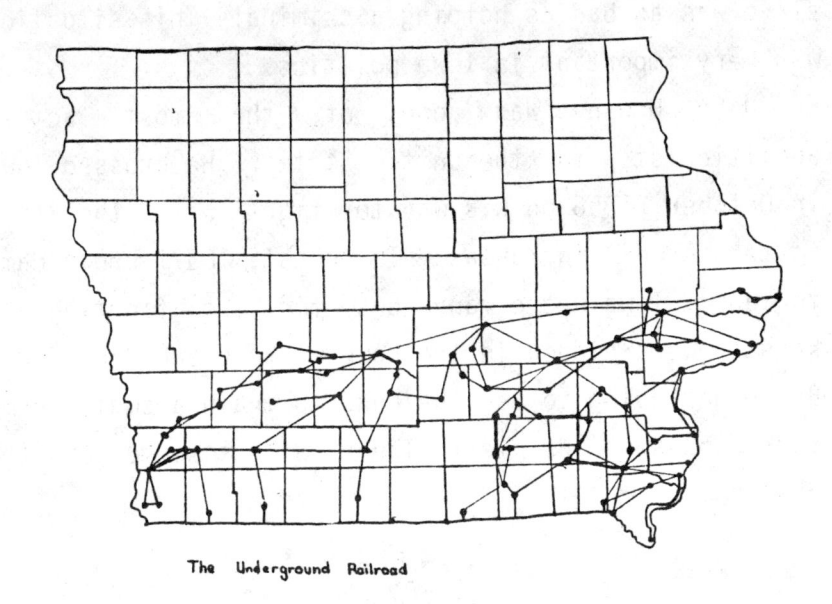

One underground railroad route led through Tabor, Earlham, Winterset, Grinnell and Springdale to Clinton. Another ran through Denmark to Burlington and a third from Denmark to Salem and Crawfordsville to Muscatine.

Many of the early Iowa settlers were from the middle and southern states. While there were people who believed in slavery, very few slaves were held in Iowa. Those that were here were only held as slaves for a short time. Legally, they could not be held at all, according to the Missouri Compromise and the state constitution.

One of the laws passed by the Territorial legislature prevented free blacks from staying in Iowa unless they paid a $500 bond as a guarantee of their good behavior. This made it almost impossible to live here. Many people also believed that aiding a runaway slave was as bad as helping a criminal. This situation was very important in Iowa politics.

John Brown was one of the most active abolitionists in the United States. He crossed Iowa in October, 1856 on his way to fight with the free state forces in Kansas. In August, 1857, Brown came to Tabor, Iowa where many guns for the fighting in Kansas were hidden in the home of Reverend John Todd. Brown was going to use the guns to train a small army for Kansas. He left Tabor with some men and the weapons.

John Brown

About the time Brown began to give up the fight in Kansas, he planned to strike a large blow in the east. He enlisted 13 men and started east. The party reached Springdale, Iowa, a Quaker settlement in Cedar county. Brown left to round up funds and support. The small army spent the winter of 1857-58 on the farm of William Maxson. They and 2 young

EDWIN and BARCLAY COPPOC

Quakers, Edwin and Barclay Coppoc of Springdale, spent the winter working on the farm and drilling like an army.

Brown returned in the summer of 1858 and took his band to Tabor. From there in the winter of 1858, they staged a raid into Missouri to free slaves. In the process, they also took horses, wagons, cattle and other property. A slave holder was also killed. By February 1859, the fugitives had worked their way back to Springdale by way of Nebraska. They were headed to Canada. Because of the stolen property and killing, the Quakers were not in sympathy this time. However, United States Marshalls were on their way to arrest Brown and his band, so William Penn Clarke of Iowa City and J. B. Grinnell of Grinnell agreed to aid them. A freight car was secured and the band made it to Canada by way of Chicago.

Brown decided to start a rebellion by capturing the federal arsenal at Harper's Ferry in Virginia. He reasoned that if the southern slaves had an adequate supply of weapons and a leader, they would rise in rebellion and overthrow their masters.

On October 6, 1859, John Brown, with about 20 men trained and equipped in Iowa, made the attack. So few men could not hope to defeat the federal army and the state of Virginia. The hoped-for rebellion never happened. John Brown was captured and hung. Edwin Coppoc, one of the Iowans from Springdale, was also captured and put to death. His brother, Barclay, escaped back to Iowa. Thus ended an episode of the frenzied abolitionist movement with an Iowa connection.

The election of Abraham Lincoln, the Republican candidate for President in 1860, was supported by a clear majority of Iowa votes. This election made it apparent to many southern states that the days of legal slavery were numbered if they stayed in the Union.

In 1861, eleven states left the union and formed their own separate government. Later that same year, some troops of the Confederate States of America, as the new government was called, fired on the Union stronghold of Ft. Sumter, South Carolina, and the Civil War began.

War was never really declared by the Union or Confederacy. Acting on his powers as commander-in-chief of the nation's armed forces, and his oath to

Animated scene outside a recruiting office. Note the inducements.

defend the country, President Lincoln called for 75,000 volunteers for 90 days. As the war went on, it created the first military draft in our history. By the end of the war, Iowa was 12,000 men over her fair share. Due to the hard times of the state, at first there were far more volunteers than the state could provide with uniforms and guns.

Governor Kirkwood wrote enthusiastically to the Secretary of War: "10 days ago we had 2 parties in this state; today we have but one and that is for the Constitution and the Union unconditionally."

So many volunteered at the first call that Iowa's quota of one regiment (1000 men) was filled to overflowing and the Governor organized two additional regiments. To the War Department, he reported: "I can raise 10,000 men in this state, but we have no arms;

GOVERNOR SAMUEL KIRKWOOD

so, for God's sake, send us some!"

Called in special session in May, 1861, the General Assembly pledged $800,000 worth of bonds--a huge sum at the time--toward the war. Many members hurried from the state house to enlist.

The state sent 75,000 volunteers into the army. This was 2/3 of the eligible men. More than one-sixth (13,000) were killed. Iowa contributed a greater percentage of eligible men to military service than any other state, North or South. 48 infantry regiments, 9 cavalry regiments and 4 artillery companies were organized during 4 years. Iowa also had many high-ranking officers in the Union army such as Curtis, Steele and Herron. Many of these men were important in the state and nation following the war.

W. W. Belknap became Secretary of War; Cyrus Bussey became Assistant Secretary of the Interior; G. M. Dodge was a power in the nationwide Union Pacific Railway.

Billy Yank.

Common soldier of the Civil War.

  Iowa troops fought in the Battle of Wilson's Creek in Missouri, Pea Ridge in Arkansas, Fort Donelson in Kentucky, Shiloh in Virginia, Chattanooga in Tennessee, and Vicksburg and Corinth in Mississippi. They also marched with Sherman to the sea. Iowa regiments were with the Union Army of the Potomac in Virginia and fought with General Sheridan in the Shenandoah Valley. Iowans died at Andersonville Prison.

  Twenty-seven Iowans won the Congressional Medal of Honor, first awarded in the Civil War.

  In addition to the regular soldiers, Iowa also organized many companies of home guards to protect the northern border from the Sioux and the southern

135

Congressional Medal of Honor

boundary from Missouri Confederate guerillas and their raids. The so-called Peace Democrats or Copperheads and other southern sympathizers worked against enlistments and the draft, often on sincere Constitutional grounds. The Knights of the Golden Circle were, it is said, organized in every township in the state, 42,000 members in all.

On one occasion, Peace Democrats paraded through South English, challenging townspeople gathered at a Republican convention. A fight broke out and Talley, leader of the Peace Democrats, was shot. Rumors flashed that a band of several thousand of his followers was readying an attack on the town.

Governor Kirkwood ordered eleven companies of the Home Guard to the scene. Faced with armed resistance and the stern governor, the Talley followers lost their thirst for revenge.

Iowa, after the Civil War, was a very different

Civil War battle scene

state. The state was rapidly changing from a frontier to a settled territory. Log cabins gave way to frame houses and the towns began to grow. The growth of railroads, immediately after the war, was dramatic as they rapidly completed the laying of rails across the state. Eastern speculators now poured large amounts of money into such Iowa industries as railroads and mills. Men from Iowa achieved a national name for themselves through the young Republican party. Some men such as G.M. Dodge came out of the war as a Major General and later was made chief engineer of the Union Pacific Railroad. Senator James Harlan, who had been serving in Congress, was appointed to President Lincoln's cabinet only a month before the president's assassination. The war left the Republican party in a position of nearly total control of the state, so much

137

Senator James Harlan

GEN. G. M. DODGE

so that Iowa became virtually a one-party state for the rest of the century.

Like many other states, one of the primary changes was the condition of the Negro. Before the war, although opposed to slavery, Iowans were not willing to accept as equals the ex-slaves. Many, like Josiah Grinnell, whose voice had been raised loudly to abolish slavery, now raised it equally loud to oppose giving blacks the right to vote. However, times were changing in Iowa, and a change in the state's constitution to give Negroes the right to vote passed by a 66% vote of white Iowans in 1868. Attitudes were changing too.

Iowa, like the rest of the nation, stood at the beginning of a new era, an era where change would shape a new world at an ever-increasing rate. The

Black males were allowed to vote for the 1st time.

railroads, retarded through lack of money during the Civil War, were the key to the growth of industry. The veterans also came back with new ideas and visions through their dealings with other parts of the country. But it was the railroad more than any other single thing that tied the country together. It not only transported manufactured goods and farm produce, but served a social purpose. People in cities and rural areas began to understand each other better. The result of this period of growth was a new unity and a better and stronger America. We will see how this resulted in changes in life in Iowa--changes that are still in motion today.

CHAPTER IX

The Civil War veterans coming home to Iowa found a state that had changed greatly from the state they had left.

Iowa was rapidly losing its frontier flavor, log cabins giving way to frame houses. Woods were being cleared for crops and the vast miles of prairie grass were plowed up to plant corn and wheat.

All over the nation new factories and mills were being built, and cities were growing. Iowans were turning their efforts away from the destruction of war toward building a better way of life with all the new machines and inventions.

Throughout the country the things such as soil, climate, geography, and location shaped different ways of business, farming and living. We will see how each region of the country grew different crops, raised different livestock, or manufactured different products. This concept is often referred to by the

CORN
COTTON
WHEAT & SMALL GRAIN

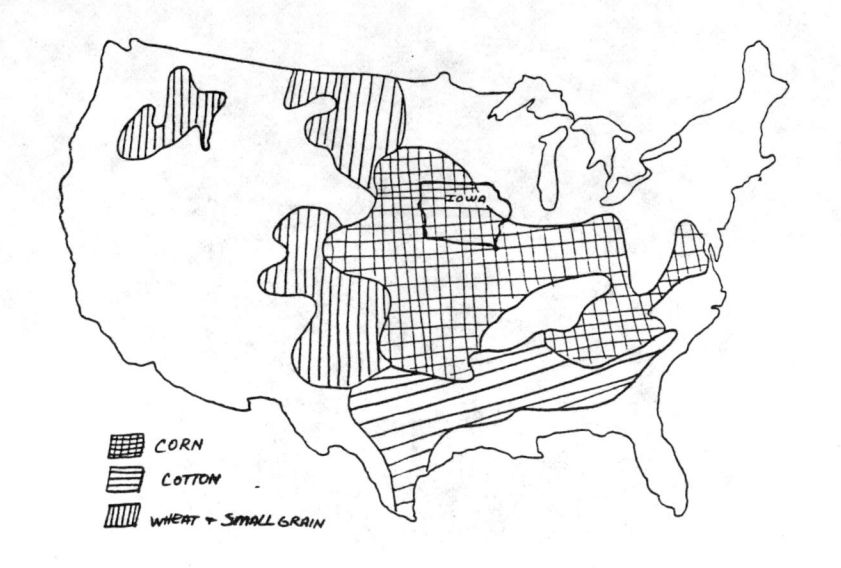

use of the term "belts". Now, for example, in Iowa, Illinois and Missouri, corn is the major crop; thus, these states are called the Corn Belt. The plains states of Nebraska, the Dakotas, Kansas and Montana raise a lot of wheat, so they are called the Wheat Belt. Both before and after the Civil War, the southern states raised a lot of cotton and became known as the Cotton Belt.

Just as crops shaped the way things were, so did minerals and rivers. In the northern states the abundance of coal and water power led to a large concentration of heavy industry. It was the machines manufactured in the eastern states of the North that would influence Iowa from this period on.

During this period, two machines were invented that were to change life in both Iowa and the nation forever. One was the McCormick Marsh Reaper which allowed the cutting and binding of wheat, allowing one

Reaper exhibited at Iowa State Fair in 1867.

man to do the work of six. The drawbacks to the early reapers were overcome in 1872 when two inventors invented twine-binding attachments. The other major invention was the sewing machine which came into use about the same time. The sewing machine was also the key to the making of clothes as a business. Soon a whole new industry had started, adding new reasons for the growth of towns and cities and the farmers' need for them. It has been said that Lincoln's Emancipation Proclamation which freed the slaves, for which a million men died, was minor in its results compared to the freedom that the world owes to the inventors of this machinery.

The years immediately following the Civil War were not good ones for most Iowans. The United States had a huge debt at the close of the Civil War. A part of the war funding had been gathered from the people by selling paper money. The bills were green on one side and called greenbacks. The regular money was gold, silver and copper coinage. After the war, Congress decided to call in these greenbacks and offered to pay their value in coins. But by withdrawing a part of the circulating money, the rest would become scarcer and farm prices would go lower. Because of this, the farmers organized the Greenback Party. In addition to other reforms, they didn't want the notes cashed in. They succeeded in keeping the notes the way they were and contributed to our present system of paper currency.

Farming was still the main business of the state and farming was not well-paying. The good market prices of war years sank to new lows as farm production increased faster than the population of towns where markets were located. This problem was made even worse by a series of natural catastrophes that made it almost impossible for farmers to keep their land.

Starting in 1867, and for the next ten years, swarms of grasshoppers attacked the land and destroyed the crops. In the worst year, 1873, the insects were so thick that their flights obscured the sun and were mistaken, by many, for clouds. Along the railroad tracks they were piled so thick that trains had to be stopped regularly because the insects acted like grease on the rails. The grasshoppers often covered twenty miles a day, and after they passed, the country looked like it had been burned by a prairie fire. The

YEAR OF THE GRASSHOPPER

damage was enormous. Many farm families were near starvation. The destruction was so complete that the state legislature had to provide $50,000 for seed to allow crops to be planted. The poor crops hit the state badly.

During those lean years not only were new settlements in Iowa halted, but thousands of people left the areas that were in trouble. The price of farm land went down fifty per cent. There were few people interested in buying even the best of farm land. Some people were in such a hurry to leave that they didn't even wait long enough to sell their land. They just left.

Even though machinery increased the amount that one man could farm, the practices of farmers of the 1860's had not changed a lot from those in use during the Revolutionary War, methods that were much like those used in Biblical times. Farmers generally

Common farmer of the 1860's.

raised only one major crop year after year, which wore out the soil. Fertilizer or crops which would enrich the soil were not used so no nutrients were returned to the soil. The farmers also used no methods that would stop soil erosion.

To understand this period, we must remember that when settlers came to Iowa, the soil was so rich and productive that all a farmer had to do was scratch the dirt, and throw in some seeds to produce what was then a great crop. There were no such things as land management or rotation of crops. Every acre not plowed was considered wasted. It is sad to note that the richness of the soil led people to waste its resources.

At the time of statehood, Iowa's major crop was wheat. It could be planted easily and yielded 40 bushels to an acre with little or no effort, which was pretty good then. Many farmers planted wheat and only wheat year after year on the same fields. What they did not know was that this one cash crop was removing

145

Cinch Bug

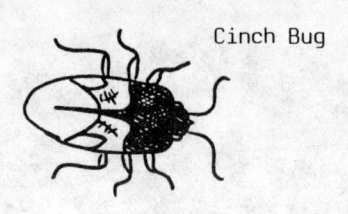

a key element from their soil - nitrogen. Without it, wheat could easily be attacked by insects. By 1879 this problem had gone so far that the wheat crop was practically wiped out by cinch bugs. Wheat yields sank to 10 bushels per acre. With failing crops, wheat farmers left the state for greener pastures, places like North and South Dakota and Kansas, states with a growing reputation for raising wheat. Hamlin Garland, a major author of the day, described the westward movement as "a stampede; hardly anything else was talked about. Every man who could sell out had gone west or was going."

The state's newspaper editors, in an effort to discourage this, ran numerous articles describing the droughts on the plains and the blizzards of the Dakotas.

As with any movement of such a large number of people, the effects were soon felt in other sectors of the population. With the departure of the wheat farmers, the flour mills in nearby towns began to suffer. Up until then, every town had produced enough wheat to keep at least one mill. Now, what had been an important part of many towns' economy, had disappeared. In some cases, this spelled the end of the town as well.

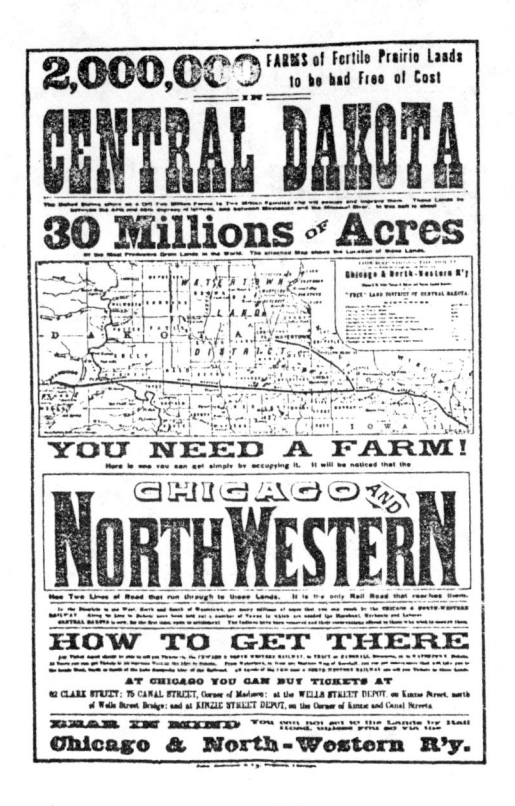

> **2,000,000** FARMS of Fertile Prairie Lands to be had Free of Cost
> **CENTRAL DAKOTA**
> **30 Millions of Acres**
> YOU NEED A FARM!
> **CHICAGO AND NorthWestern**
> HOW TO GET THERE
> **Chicago & North-Western R'y.**

In order to combat this emergency, the state legislature appointed a commission in 1870 to promote immigration from other countries. This was so successful that by 1880 most of the empty land caused by the exodus of the wheat farmers had been filled with German and Scandinavian immigrants. So important to the development of the state was this immigration that the commission printed 65,000 copies of "Iowa: The Home for Immigrants" in 5 languages. The book provided social, economic and geographical information about the state. These were distributed in the eastern states and Europe. The book proclaimed Iowa as one of the healthiest and one of the best watered states. It also said that Iowa had fewer criminals

IOWA:

THE HOME FOR IMMIGRANTS,

BEING A

TREATISE ON THE RESOURCES OF IOWA.

AND

GIVING USEFUL INFORMATION WITH REGARD TO
THE STATE, FOR THE BENEFIT OF
IMMIGRANTS AND OTHERS.

PUBLISHED BY ORDER OF THE

IOWA BOARD OF IMMIGRATION.

DES MOINES:
MILLS & CO., PRINTERS AND PUBLISHERS.
1870.

and poor people because of the great opportunities offered by the region.

Another important method of encouraging immigration was the "America letters" which foreigners already in the state sent to their relatives at home. A satisfied immigrant would write back to his friends and relatives telling them how wonderful Iowa was. These happy letters would usually result in those friends or relatives also coming to this country and Iowa.

To the common people of Europe who had very little chance of improving their lives or acquiring land,

Group of immigrants

Iowa was a great opportunity. In addition, Iowa was tolerant of religious and political beliefs and impressed no one into the military. It seemed like a fairy tale when a person could buy cheap land, many times on credit, and practice his religion as he pleased provided he observed common decency. Compared with the wages paid in Iowa, particularly during the period of railroad construction, the wages paid in Europe were extremely low. By a few years of self-denial, people coming to Iowa could realize the dream that only a very few Europeans could hope to fulfill on that continent.

By 1870, 18 percent of Iowa's residents were foreign-born. Germans ranked highest with Irish, English, Swedish, Danish and Norwegians ranking next. Generally the foreign-born settled in northern Iowa and along the Mississippi. Immigrants from the same

1.4%	Danish
1.5%	French
2%	Swiss
2%	Dutch
3%	Scottish
5%	Swedish
8%	English
9%	Norwegian
20%	Irish
32%	German

country often grouped together in particular areas. Even today, some towns have very strong characteristics of their ethnic heritage.

These new citizens applied new methods and new ways. They made use of recent inventions that would change life in the prairie states forever.

One such invention was the cream separator, invented in 1880 by a Swede named DeLaval. This machine separated cream from milk which allowed milk to be transported in large amounts. Before this, the milk had to set for 24 hours. Therefore, much of it

The cream separator was invented in 1880.

Creamery

turned sour. This made for a small and unprofitable industry. A creamery is a central station where milk is brought to make butter. Creameries were one of Iowa's first large industries. In this case, the product they made or manufactured was butter and cream. The first creameries were started by John Steward in Manchester and H. D. Sherman in Monticello. It was at such an establishment, near Strawberry Point, that the famous Pride of Iowa Butter was made that won a gold ribbon at the Philadelphia Exhibition in 1876. This prize won Iowa national attention as a dairy state and soon creameries were springing up all over the state. By 1880, it is estimated that one-third of all the butter made in the U.S. was made in Iowa. A wealth never dreamed of by the wheat growers poured into the state. The richness of the soil that had been exhausted by the grain growers was restored and even multiplied by the butter makers through their planting of hay and other forage crops.

The problems of the 60's and 70's, agriculturally damaging though they were, did start some long-lasting changes.

With grain prices so low farmers turned to feeding their corn to cattle and hogs. These animals were fattened and driven to the nearest town with a railroad stop. They were then shipped to the slaughter houses of Chicago. During these years, with so many animals shipped to the stockyards by rail, Chicago gained a name for itself as the "hog butcher of the world". In fact, railroads made much of Iowa's agricultural growth possible by providing a means to ship out its products.

Train in Southern Iowa about 1870

The great lesson Iowa farmers learned was to do more than one major thing at a time, such as raising animals and crops to sell. The idea of raising several crops and feeding some of those crops to livestock was the key to success. Agricultural leaders of the era instructed their followers not to put their faith in one cash crop, but to raise others, and to raise several kinds of livestock. What was to become known as a "feedlot economy" was beginning.

"Raise corn always in preference to wheat. Learn to change corn to beef, pork and meat by the cheapest and least expensive ways."

"Diversify agriculture and leave wheat raising to our young pioneers on virgin soil and to farmers who are close to railroads."

A packing house.

The idea of feeding grain to livestock for shipment to packing houses changed Iowa. The western large cattle and sheep ranchers of the 1860's gave way to purebred hog and cattle farms of the Midwest. The number of hogs and cattle increased rapidly. In the decade of the 1870's, farmers were said to have "hog mania", as Iowa led the nation in swine population. During the following ten years, cattle numbers rapidly increased, especially the purebreds hereford, angus and shorthorn. With so many cattle and hogs to feed,

153

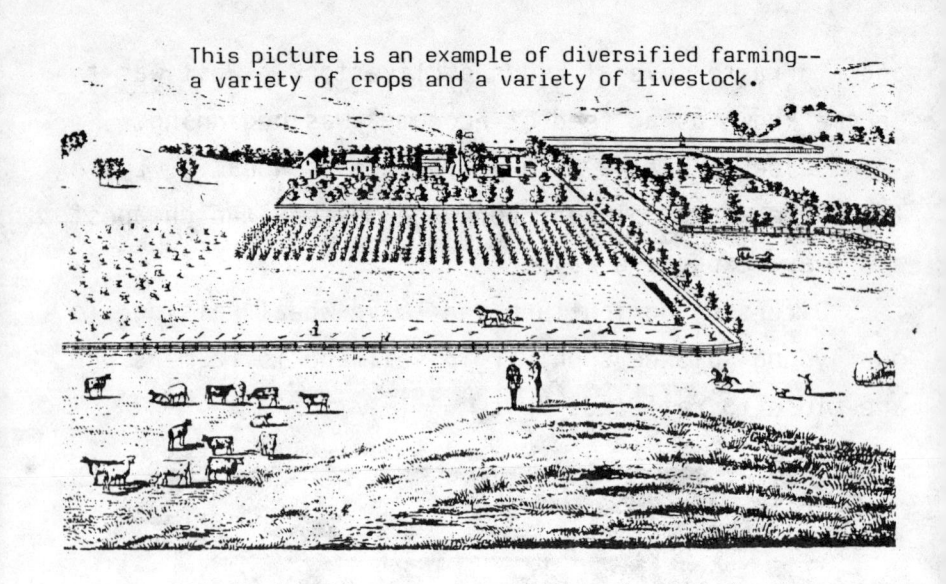

This picture is an example of diversified farming-- a variety of crops and a variety of livestock.

it was only natural that corn would become the chief crop of the state. By 1879, Iowa was the second largest producer of corn in the nation. Within ten years, it was number one.

Farmers began to rotate their crops. This is the practice of raising different crops on the same land in alternate years. In Iowa, it was common to plant corn in a field one year, and oats the next. Thus it was that 1879 also saw Iowa as the U.S.'s number one producer of oats as well as corn, a position it still holds today. The following year, the state Secretary of Agriculture described corn as "the staple crop of the state".

As a sidelight of this crop rotation, the production of quality oats attracted industry. George Douglas brought to Cedar Rapids the Scotch method of processing oats. By 1875, a seven story building had been erected and the plant could process 600 barrels of oats per day. This was the start of the world-famous Quaker Oats Company.

Up until this time in Iowa's history, the Iowa soil was so productive that the pioneers paid little attention to the conservation of its fertility. Smaller yields and soil depletion forced the farmer to recognize that something needed to be done. Crop rotation was not the only answer. Farmers started to use fertilizers and drainage. Instead of leaving old straw and barnyard manure to rot around the barns, the barnyard wastes were spread on the fields. Ditching and tiling also improved the land. Large areas of marsh land has since been turned into productive farm lands through these methods.

With all the cattle and hogs being raised, there was a tremendous need for local packing houses, especially in those parts of the state not served efficiently by railroads. For example, by 1880, the Sioux City Packing House was one of the five largest in the country.

The lesson of diversity has been long remembered and practiced. Only since the mid-20th Century have specialized farms begun to predominate the Iowa agricultural picture.

When people go through times as hard as the 1860's and 1870's were, they often feel the need to blame their misfortunes on someone else. In this period, the group that was blamed the most were the railroad owners. Even though the farmers' misfortunes weren't all the fault of the railroads, the railroad rates

Railroad horse

were a major reason the farmers had such a hard time making ends meet.

The controversy that arose between the farmers and their representatives and the railroad men became one of the major political and economic issues of this period.

From the first train ride from Davenport to Walcott in 1855, Iowans saw the development of the railroad as the key to their prosperity. After the war, with the financial support of East-West investors, many miles of track were laid, crossing the state from Davenport to Council Bluffs in 1867. The trans-continental railroad was completed just two years later. Iowa was now linked by rail to the rest of the country. Railroad owners told farmers that the railroad would provide an expanded market which would raise the value of farm products. Therefore, despite many hardships, farm production did increase in many areas of the state, but the promised markets weren't there. Towns and cities had not grown as fast as the farmer's production. Railroads had not yet reached the more remote, less populated areas of the state, depriving the farmers there of the expanded shipping services. Prices paid for produce were so low after the war that after farmers paid the freight rates, there was little profit left.

It soon became apparent to the general population that railroads were built to make money for their investors and owners, not for the public good. Since there were no laws governing how much they could charge their customers, railroads could raise their rates whenever they wished. In many cases, railroad owners made deals with certain shippers and towns so that in some cases shipping the items from Mason City to Des Moines cost more than shipping the same items from Des Moines to Chicago.

157

A Grange meeting

One reaction to the deals of the railroads and low farm prices was the start of an organization known originally as the Patrons of Husbandry. In the west, the organization became known as the Granger Movement. Though the organization began in the District of Columbia, it soon became very popular with Iowa farm families. By 1872, there were more than 500 Granges, as the local units were called, in Iowa. The main objective of the Grange was to promote cooperation between farm families. Soon the Grangers were trying out new ideas to solve their problems. They established cooperative stores, elevators and workhouses, many of which are still in operation today. Their organized opposition to railroad rates led to the passage of laws regulating railroad rates in Iowa. These laws were referred to as "Granger Laws". The Grange became so powerful that both political parties and newspapers began to pay heed to the Granger's opinions.

Politics were important, but more than anything else, the movement got farmers together to exchange knowledge and new advances in farming practices. People began to know more about purebred livestock and crop rotation. Rural life became less isolated, with the meetings stimulating the social life as well as the mind. This activity, combined with the change in county fairs where the newest and best in livestock and machinery was displayed, began to change opinions about the new ways. More and more farmers stopped laughing at modern agriculture ideas as "book farming".

Iowa State Agricultural College was built in Ames in 1868.

Modern agriculture had been given professional help with the opening of the State Horticultural Society in 1866 and the State Agricultural College in Ames in 1868. Even so, it took the hard years of the 60's and 70's to make farmers see that a change in agricultural practice was needed and could be helpful.

New methods were also being spread by a growing number of newspaper editors, many devoted to better farming practices. Many of them were farmers as well as newspaper men. Such men were pioneers in what became known as livestock journalism. The best known of these were James H. Sanders of Sigourney, who began publishing the Western Stock Journal, and Coker F. Clarkson of Des Moines. Mr. Clarkson's paper, the State Register, grew into the present Des Moines Register, the most powerful and listened-to publication in both agriculture and politics in the state about the same time "Uncle" Henry C. Wallace was publishing Wallaces Farmer, one of the most respected papers in the Midwest.

By 1880, with a few good crop years behind them and reasonable prices now being paid, Iowa farmers began to stay on the land, making improvements and buying more modern machinery. Again they were aided by a recent invention. It is a very good example of how small details change the world. In this case it

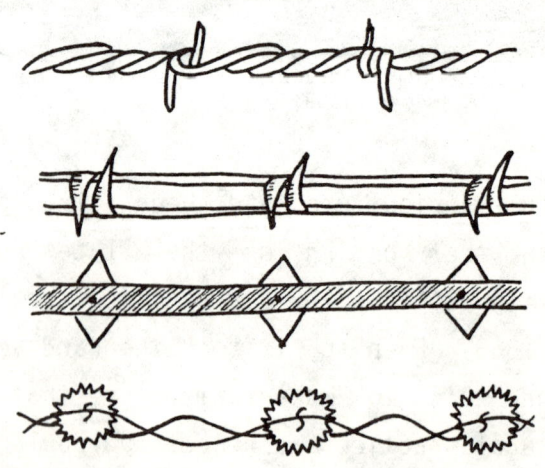

Different types of barbed wire.

was barbed wire. Even though it had been invented in 1874, it had not become available on a large scale until after a machine had been built to make it. In this way, the cost was more within the reach of the average farmer. What had been the dream of settlers on the plains, low cost fencing material became a reality in the 1880's. Not only did the fences aid in the farming of vast range of prairie, but they were further reason for raising purebred livestock. Now animal breeding could be controlled.

While it is true that agriculture was the most important subject on the minds of Iowans in this period, there were a number of changes being made that were altering the face of the young state.

Aside from the richness of the soil, Iowa possessed many other natural resources-- primary among them was coal. With the completion of railroad lines, Iowa coal could be shipped to the industrial states of the East. Coal was also used as fuel for the growing industries of Iowa. By the end of the Civil War, the state was producing 100,000 tons every year. Mining increased rapidly in the 70's. By 1880, Mahaska County alone was turning out 900,000 tons a year. This meant wealth for the state, but it also brought more people to the state. Many newly freed Negroes were coming to Iowa to fill the need for miners. One of the largest mining towns in Iowa was Buxton in Monroe County which had over 3,000 blacks. Coal mining continued to increase until after the turn of the century.

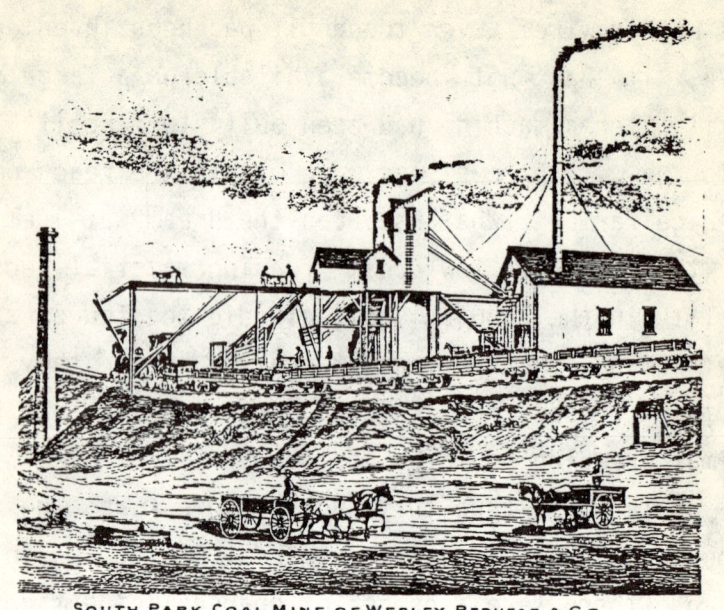

SOUTH PARK COAL MINE OF WESLEY REDHEAD & CO.
DES MOINES, IOWA — CAPACITY 300 TONS PER DAY

In this period there were many who cared more for morals than for railroads or money. These people made the liquor laws of the state their main target. After many years of public debate, non-drinking groups finally succeeded in moving the Republican party's platform. In 1882, this law of prohibition became the law of the state. Prohibition was so popular in Iowa that in 1883, the winning candidate for lieutenant governor, Orlando Manning, coined a phrase that was to become a state slogan, "A school house on every hill, and no saloon in the valley."

One state historian, Cyremus Cole, put the issue and the period in true perspective. "Who cares today about the seller of whiskey, whose arrest in 1887 threw the state into an uproar? And who cares now that men were tarred and feathered or shot down in the

The Serpent of Destruction

streets for attempting to force laws that others did not like? And as for the results of the big economic battles, have not the railroad rates and regulations that were then achieved all been stamped out by world events that no one then dreamed of in Iowa or certainly think of being a part of? But then, they were of so much importance that men were defeated for governor and even president over them."

With the return of profitable prices for crops and livestock, and a growing amount of industrial and mineral wealth, Iowans began to prosper in the late 1880's as never before. Throughout the state, as the nation, there was an air of optimism that the best times were here and should be celebrated.

163

The fabulous Corn Palace attracted worldwide attention during the five years of its existence.

    Iowans, like many other Americans, began to think of ways to show the rest of the world what their state had that was biggest or best. These displays featured the state's best resources. From 1887 to 1892, a succession of "Palaces" were built to publicize that Iowa was not only modern in every way, but to show that Iowa could compare to the fabulous exhibitions of the East.

    It began with the Corn Palaces of Sioux City and was continued with the Coal Palaces of Ottumwa and the Bluegrass Palace of Creston. Each town displayed a major resource of its' part of the state.

    As Iowans entered the 1890's, they could hardly realize what the years to come would bring. The fact was that each year that passed brought them closer and closer to the rest of the world. Soon there would not be a world event, good or bad, that would not have

164

meaning and effect in Iowa. Such things as wars or depressions far away, in parts of the world that no one had ever heard of, would soon leave their mark on the state. The human feelings toward rapid industrial growth where some machines became more important than the men who operated them would soon raise a large number of human rights issues. Iowa was no longer separated from the rest of the world. By 1890, Iowa was a part of it.

The next wave of change and problems that awaited the population in the coming years, a wave that would change the way we live today, was still to come.

CHAPTER X

After 1890, we enter a period of history in which the cause of change becomes more and more complicated. Change itself happens at an ever increasing rate.

Events do not occur in a neat order, one after another, but happen in groups, all at once. The fate of the state no longer was controlled by the forces within the borders of Iowa, but now was changed by events far from the statehouse in Des Moines. The farmers near Cedar Falls, Bloomfield, Creston, Council Bluffs and Rock Falls soon found out that what happened in Europe would dictate whether prices for corn went up or down, and, whether they would sell their milk, or pour it in a ditch.

At this time, as never before, the economic principles of our money-making society can be clearly seen. For such an economic system to prosper, there are three main ingredients: (1) goods or services, (2) a demand or need for them, and (3) something of value, such as money, to exchange. Thus, farmers who raise wheat, for example, sell it to the flour mill, receive money, which allows them to pay for their land, seed, fertilizer, machinery, and raise more wheat. The cost of these items is called the cost of production. The greater the difference between the selling price for the wheat and the cost of production, the more profit or loss for the farmer. The more people who buy wheat, the more demand there is for it, which causes the price to go up. Thus, the demand for a product tells how much money that product is worth. This rule is referred to as the "law of supply and demand". It is often called the "backbone of the free enterprise system", which is what we call our economic system. In this period, we will see great national, even world, changes in the supply and demand for food. This fact was to have an effect on the success of Iowa as never before. For instance, if England decides to buy Iowa corn and demands a lot of it, farmers will buy more land to raise crops. If the next year the English decide not to buy so much, the farmer has extra and must sell it cheaper to get rid of it because he must pay for the land and the crops he produced. A bad crop in England would make the English buy more, thereby affecting the Iowa farmer.

    This was a time filled with high hopes and great dreams, the beginning of what some call "the modern era". It was also the end of many forces that had controlled the state, country and the world for generations. This period would spell the end, not

167

An early telephone

only for many of the royal families that ruled Europe, but for the long-term political leaders of Iowa. In agriculture, the change was the result of years of mechanical and scientific advances, increases in agricultural production and land buying and selling.

The once lonely or isolated life of the farm families disappeared as the invention of the telephone soon brought a spread of wires across the state; by 1920, 86 percent of the state's population had telephones. The start of rural free delivery of mail brought the rest of the world still nearer. The first three routes began in 1896, but rapidly grew to 292 routes by 1901. The telephone and mail delivery drew the farmer closer to any help or information he might need.

In cities and towns industries that processed such agricultural products as grain, meat, milk, butter and lumber were growing. With the railroad to ship out the produce to the rest of the world, prices and land values rose, giving farmers more money to buy machinery and the manufactured goods of the cities.

Even though the period as a whole was one of the most prosperous in our history, it did not begin very well. The high prices of the 1880's soon fell, and with them went much of the state's success and good times. By 1893, the entire nation was in the worst industrial depression that had ever happened in the United States. It was called the "Panic of 1893". It began in 1893, but continued in some parts of the country until 1897.

Cyremus Cole, a newspaper editor at the time, commented: "The evidence of the panic was everywhere." Gold was no longer used and credit became scarce. Factories closed and farm product sales went down in price, far below the cost of production. In cities, men could obtain neither work nor wages; souphouses and bread lines were the order of the day. Even though products became cheaper, they were harder to get, for people had no money. Many banks closed their doors; even great businesses, including railroads, went broke because of lack of business and money.

1893 was a lean and hungry one, perhaps the leanest and poorest in the history of the state. It was the year of a great drought. In many parts of the state that summer, no rain fell for two months. As the result, there was a partial crop failure. The corn yield was cut in half. There was not enough corn to fatten the hogs for market, nor enough food to carry the cattle and horses through the winter months. As a result, cattle and hogs were rushed to markets where there was no demand for them, and where the prices were low. Good horses sold for $50.00, many for $20.00, where before they would have sold for two or three times that amount. Some of the older and more useless animals were killed to save them from starvation.

Increasing numbers of unemployed in the nation's cities banded together and became marching armies.

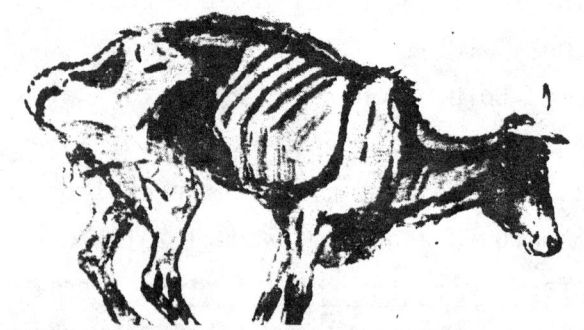

1893 was a very poor year, and alot of livestock died from starvation.

Some people called these groups "organized tramps," but the members used the term "commonwealth armies." Their destination became Washington, D.C. They were going to storm the national capital for relief.

One of the largest of these armies came into being in San Francisco early in 1894, and in its eastward march reached Iowa in the summer of that year, with over 1,000 men. Its leader was a man who was called "General Kelley." The most alarming reports preceded the march of this group. Some feared fights and trouble along the way, as the group was to enter the more populated parts of the state.

Iowa's governor, Frank Jackson, after a lot of thought and conversation allowed the men to cross the state to Des Moines and finally, on rafts, down the Des Moines river to the Mississippi. Kelley's Army was one of the few events Iowans had that year to keep their minds off their problems.

This period had scarcely begun when Iowans were asked to fight in their first overseas war. With the

A Spanish American War battle.

bombing of the United States battleship, Maine, on February 15, 1898, the U.S. Congress soon declared war on Spain. Iowans, as usual, were ready to serve. Of the four Iowa regiments, only one actually got to Cuba. They were only there during the winter of 1898. The United States won every battle and the war ended in 1899. Of the 5,000 Iowans who signed up, 163 died. Of them, only one was lost in battle--the rest died from tropical diseases such as malaria.

Horace Boies

The fact that a Democrat, Horace Boies, was elected governor of Iowa not only in 1889, but again in 1892, says a lot about the state's Republican party. After all, didn't the long-term Republican senator, Jonathan Dolliver, say with confidence that "Hell would go Methodist before Iowans went Democratic"? Obviously, something had changed.

This was not to say that the election of the Democratic governor in 1892, marked the end of the Republican party's control of the state. Far from it. The record shows that after Boies, there is not another major Democratic upset until 1932. The Democrats came to power in 1892 not only because of their promises of relief from the economic hardships, but also because of prohibition. Even though Iowa had passed such a law prohibiting the manufacture and sale of alcoholic beverages in Iowa five years before Boies election, the question was far from settled. There were other factors as well.

With the drought, low farm income and the resulting hard times, many Americans, Iowans included, were ready for a new political party. Iowa, as were part of the western states and the states of the south, was among regions of greatest hurt and least security. In these areas, current economic and agricultural problems created a demand for political change. It was an idea that had some beginnings in Iowa, but soon spread to the rest of the country.

The Republican party, due to their image of being pro-railroads, lost much of the support of the state's farmers. It also should be pointed out that Boies had been a Republican, but left the party mainly over the issue of prohibition, which Republicans had long supported. Even more important was the gradual change during this period in the leadership of the Iowa Republican party.

Since before the Civil War, the party had been run by a small group of businessmen who didn't like change, and later, Civil War veterans, often referred to as "the regency". Since they could control who was nominated by the party, and since a Republican nomination was almost the same as being elected, "the regency" in effect controlled the state. After Boies was defeated in his bid for a third term in 1896, the state elected the last in a long line of these Civil War veterans, Governor Frances Drake. Along with Drake's election, Iowa returned to solidly supporting the Republican party. But many of the leaders like Drake were getting on in years, and by the end of 1916, many of them were dead. At the same time, and since the early 1890's, a group of younger men more in favor of change began to seek control of the party. These men were known as progressives. Progressives believed that there was need for change in government and society. Conservatives wanted to keep things as they were, sometimes referred to as the status quo or even a return to the "good old days". In some cases these progressives formed other political parties such as the Progressive party or the Green Back party.

Populism, or the People's party, was especially active in the west and south. Iowa had a great many

JAMES B. WEAVER,
CANDIDATE FOR PRESIDENT

who believed in these parties. One of the People's party most famous leaders was General James Baird Weaver. After having served a term in Congress, he was nominated for president by the national Greenback party in 1880 and again by the Populists in 1892. During the campaigns, he gained great popularity with the common people in both the north and south.

Probably the best known of the older statesmen during this era was William Allison of Dubuque. He served in the Iowa House of Representatives before he was chosen to serve in the United States Senate in 1872. Allison served there until 1908. During that time he turned down many national cabinet positions. In 1888, Allison was one of the leaders for the Republican nomination for president.

By the turn of the century, the progressive wing of the Republican Party had enough support to nominate, and thus elect, one of its own - Albert Cummins, as the state's governor. Cummins and the progressives continued to gain influence, and in 1907

Barracks, Fort Des Moines, Iowa

succeeded in convincing the Iowa legislature to pass the Direct Primary Law. This reform had been attempted several times before. The law established a primary election on the first Monday in June of the even-numbered years. Each party who met the requirements would select its official candidates for all county and state offices, except judges, for representatives in Congress and in the Senate from those in each party who wished to be considered for the office. The bill's backers claimed that this would move the nominating process out of the backrooms and put it in the hands of the mass public, where it belonged. Even though Iowans were among the leaders of progressive politics, including the women's right to vote movement, many still did not want to change.

The easy-going attitude of the Hawkeye state was due in part to greater well-being and safety, both with money and crops. States farther west did not

Women's Sufferage Movement

The windmill was invented in the mid 1890's.

enjoy the same degree of well-being. Equally important was the confidence, in the midst of falling prices and "temporarily" failing crops, that "normal" seasons would soon return, and that in a growing nation, the demand for food encouraged producing as much as possible. Reports of county agricultural people in the drought years expressed confidence that the drought would not happen again in Iowa and not in their county in particular. "Warren County is indeed prosperous. We heard of the return of prosperity, but it is a fact that Warren County never lost her prosperity." According to the reports, future bumper crops were not only likely, but a thing to bank on."

Fortunately, this faith and high feeling was not to be put to too long a strain. Better seasons, rising prices, and the catching up of demand with output, modern machines, and the growth of credit programs were bringing a "new prosperity". By the turn

177

of the century, even the western farmer was sharing this prosperity. Certainly no others were in a better position to profit by the returning good times and more opportunities, material and social, than the farmers living in the heart of the corn belt. As one speaker at a corn carnival in 1899 said, "Gentlemen, from the beginning of Indiana to the end of Nebraska, there is nothing but corn, cattle and contentment."

Iowa's governor, Leslie Shaw, in 1900 said proudly, "The future of agriculture, therefore the future of Iowa, is most promising. A quarter of a century later, or perhaps less, the population of the United States will be enough to eat up the present annual production of our farms."

The period from 1897 to 1920 is often referred to by many historians as "the Golden Age of Agriculture". This means that during those years, the profits that the average farmer earned on crops and livestock rose at a much higher rate than the cost of production, that is money spent on machinery, seed, and fertilizer. This relationship between market prices and the cost of production is often referred to as "parity". Farmers often state that they want to achieve parity, that is, to sell their products for what it cost the farmer to produce them plus a profit.

As farm prices rose, many farmers rushed out to buy more land, more equipment and more fertilizer. They raised bigger crops and better meat animals, produced more milk and butter and raked in the profits, giving little heed to what tomorrow might bring. A farm crisis was in the making.

The farmers came to rely on the huge foreign market. They produced as much as they could. The rest of the world was catching up in technology and opening new farm lands. Pioneer countries such as Canada, Argentina and Australia were starting to produce. The American grain grower and stockman could no longer compete because of shipping costs, foreign taxes and cost of production. At the same time, the foreign market was shrinking. European countries made a practice of buying food from their own colonies.

The purchases of foreign countries at this time caused a final spurt.

For several years the drop in the amount of exports, large though it was, was not seriously felt. The spreading population of the cities and factories continued to grow. A city population working in factories, and with quite a bit of money, must eat.

As historian Leland Sage explained, "Iowa's factories and cities, then and later, would be keyed to her agricultural economy." After the turn of the century gasoline machines began to replace manpower, horsepower, and even steam powered machines, in farms in Europe and America, no where more than in Iowa. Steam engines, both stationary and portable had long been used to do farm work, but portable steam engines had many handicaps: proper fuel was sometimes difficult to obtain, sometimes water had to be hauled great distances, and worst of all, the monsters might bog down in a wet field. As a result of these short-

One of the first tractors.

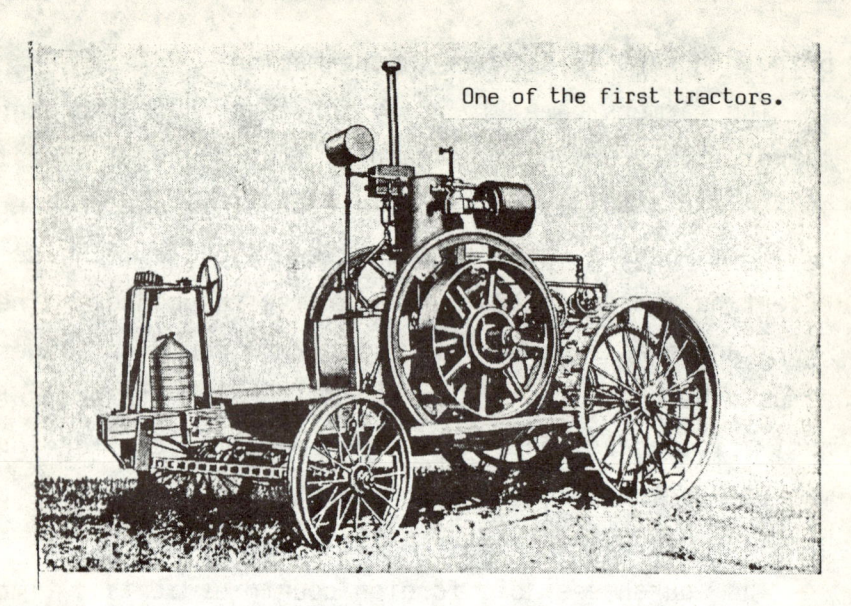

comings, various manufacturing firms experimented with gas engines, but none could overcome the problems. In 1892, John Froelich, a farmer-tinkerer in Clayton County, succeeded in harnessing a Van Dusen engine to a farm implement and made it move forward and in reverse. He perhaps did not realize the extent of the revolution he had launched.

The introduction of the gasoline powered tractor was one of the most important events in the history of American agriculture.

The advantages that the tractor had over horses or mules for field work was its greater speed and that it required no rest period. The tractor needed to be stopped only for adding oil or gasoline or for repairs. With a belt attached, it could power a wood saw, feed grinder or water pump. Use of the tractor grew quickly after it was once accepted by farmers. The 1910 U.S. census indicated 10,000 tractors in the

U.S. on farms. In ten years there would be nearly 1/4 of a million.

Use of gasoline powered tractors for farm work solved some of the farmers' problems, but at the same time brought new ones. No longer would he raise the feed for horses and mules which furnished power for farm work. Instead, he bought fuel, oil, and grease for his tractor. This marked the end of the farm that could survive all by itself. Larger farms used the tractor and tractor operated machinery to the best advantage, and smaller farms were sold to large farm operators. In turn, this affected small towns, with fewer farm operations to support businesses in a town and fewer laborers needed from the towns during the harvest seasons. This produced some very important results.

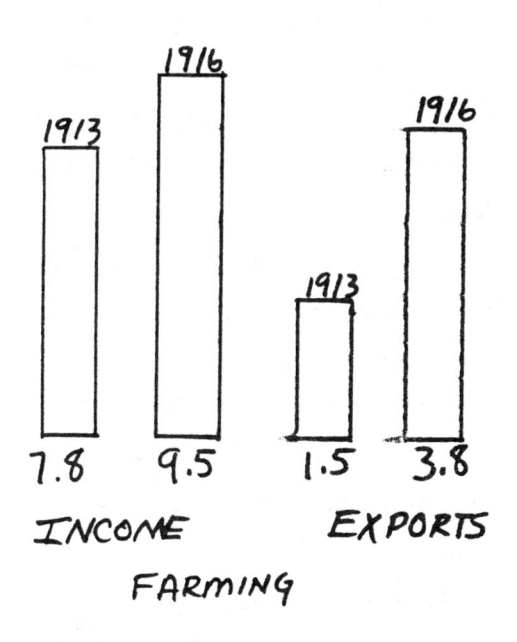

	1913	1916
INCOME FARMING	7.8	9.5
EXPORTS	1.5	3.8

One result of this labor shift was the fact that for the only time in our history, the population of Iowa went down. From 1900 to 1910, in the 99 counties, the population of 71 went down, while 28, mostly with larger cities, made gains. As small farmers sold out to larger ones, and as fewer farm hands were needed, the people moved to larger cities, or to other states. Some experts also give credit to the attraction of cheaper land in states further west and in Canada. These experts also point out that factory employment did not grow nearly as fast as farm unemployment. Farm income shot upward, from $7.8 billion in 1913 to $9.5 billion in 1916. American exports also rose from $1.5 billion to $3.8 billion in 1916.

It sounds odd to say, but the Golden Age of Agriculture might have ended in 1913 had it not been for the coming of World War I. "Well before 1914, American farmers were producing surpluses of some crops and there was talk of reducing excesses of supply over demand. The war in Europe rescued the whole American economy, especially the agricultural section, from a noticeable decline in 1914. By 1915, Europe's misfortune was bringing a noticeable prosperity to Americans, which America's entry into the war in 1917 merely served to increase. This unexpected turn of events prevented dealing with the problem of surpluses while it was in the early stages. After the war, American farmers were keyed to a policy of all-out production when full production was no longer needed."

Since before the election of Woodrow Wilson as President in 1912, American government had followed a course of neutrality in most matters for foreign policy, especially in Europe. Neutrality means that a country doesn't want to take sides in arguments that various foreign governments are having with each other. This policy was becoming more and more difficult after 1910, as American interests abroad were threatened. By 1914, the U.S. was shipping both arms and food to the allied nations of Europe. These included England, France, Belgium, Russia, Serbia and Italy.

After the sinking of the Lusitania by a German submarine in 1915, which killed 114 Americans, President Wilson was under increasing pressure to strike back against Germany. The last straw came in 1917 when the German Ambassador to the U.S. announced that Germany would not spare American ships on the sea from their submarine attacks around Great Britain. On

"ALLIED NATIONS"
GREAT BRITAIN
FRANCE
ITALY
RUSSIA
SERBIA
ROMANIA

183

February 3rd, America broke off political relations with Germany. On April 2nd, President Wilson asked the Congress to declare war, and on April 6th, Congress did just that and declared war on Germany and Austria-Hungary. The U.S. thus joined the side of what was called the "Allied Nations". Our part in what was called "the war to end all wars" and "the war to make the world safe for democracy" had begun.

As with the rest of the nation, Iowans supported and freely took part in the war effort. Out of the population of 2,400,000 people, with half of that being male, 113,000 between 21 and 31 registered for military duty under the selective services or draft act. Army posts were established at Camp Dodge and Fort Des Moines. Fort Des Moines was to become the only training camp in the country for black officers in an army which said blacks and whites couldn't mix. Within eight months after Congress declared war, Iowans were in France as part of the American Army.

Albert B. Cummins

"Food will win the war" was now the saying heard and seen everywhere. The U.S. government made loans to Allied Europe which allowed them to buy American produce in huge quantities. All this meant money to farmers. Governmental spokesmen urged farmers in Iowa, as in other states, to produce to the limit, and bankers begged them to borrow more money to buy more land for this purpose. Experts showed the farmers how to increase low yields and urged them to plow up pasture and roadsides and put these areas into production.

No one could lose, it seemed, even if the price of land did shoot up to $800 to $1000 an acre. A farmer could make a down payment, mortgage the farm for the balance and in a few good years, pay off the debt. What with wheat selling for $2.20 to $3.60 per bushel, and corn at $2.00 to $3.00, Iowa farmers never had it so good.

As usual, with the high prices, agricultural production increased greatly. Increase that had begun before 1914 continued, so that by 1919, both cattle and hogs had reached all-time highs. More corn and wheat were planted on more acres than ever before. The average value for a farm in Iowa grew as well from

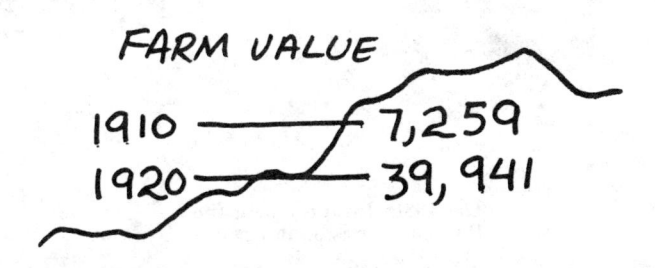

FARM VALUE
1910 —— 7,259
1920 —— 39,941

185

$7,259 in 1910 to $39,941 in 1920, or nearly 5 1/2 times. As land prices went up, so did the debts of farmers buying land. In the same ten year period, the money that the state's farmers owed doubled.

All in all, farm production did play an important role in helping to win the war. As Secretary of Agriculture Houston pointed out in 1918, "During the war, America helped Europe save civilization by making large supplies of food stuffs available to the Allies. It did this through increased production and conservation." But for this help, it is difficult to see how the allies could have waged war and won.

Iowa's farmers helped, but so did her soldiers. Of all the Iowans united in the armed forces, surely the most famous was the Rainbow Division's 168th Infantry. The first Iowan to die in World War I was also one of the first three Americans killed in the war: Merle Hay of Glidden. By the end of the war,

The 168th Infantry with the Rainbow Division in France

A World War I soldier

with the Armistice of 1918, over 2000 Iowans had died serving their country in active duty.

As soon as the war ended, President Wilson ordered an immediate return to regular business, but exceptions had to be made. The government had been supporting farm prices by paying additional money for food. Price supports for American farm products stayed through 1919 and well into 1920, and loans to some foreign countries were continued. This special period was a help to all and should have provided a cushion for those who were still producing too much. Wallace's Farmer urged its farm readers to "back down the ladder a rung at a time" or to cut back, and warned them that farmers would be the first "to be pushed off the ladder." Yet it seemed to come as a surprise when public announcement was made May 31,

187

1920, that the guaranteed war price on wheat was withdrawn and supports under other crops would soon go the same way. Because not as much food was needed, prices would go down unless production was decreased. Loans to European countries were shut off at the same time.

It seems, in looking back, that the government officials and farmers made every possible mistake in dealing with the problem of doing away with the war programs. Without loans, the European nations were still making post-war changes and could no longer pay American prices that had been rising since 1914 because of the demand. The products that were being sent to other countries, which had been the key to our good fortune on the farm, now continued in the same or even a slightly higher level, but at only half the former prices. If demand for food is high, prices will be high. If demand goes down and production doesn't, prices will be low.

Even before the farm crash of 1920, farm income had dropped about 50% and now, just when the American farmer needed credit to carry him over this rough spot, the Federal Reserve Board raised the loan rate. Money tightened up, the county banks could not renew the notes of their customers, and mortgages came due at the very worst time. To add to the farmer's problems, the Esch-Cummins Act of 1920 allowed an increase in freight rates, taking a larger slice out of the farmers' income which was rapidly getting smaller.

Foreclosure sales left farmers indigent— a fate worse than that of city paupers.

Most cruel of all, the farmer found that prices and wages in other parts of the economy were holding up, while prices he received were going down. This loss of purchasing power, soon to be expressed as "the loss of parity of income", was the knockout blow. Many a farmer who had followed the advice of the government and his banker to increase his acreage, now found that his only relief was through bankruptcy. Being bankrupt is when you have no money and cannot pay those you owe. Whereas in 1914, only 5 1/2 percent of such cases involved farmers, by 1920 that national figure had almost tripled.

Despite heading for a full scale depression, Iowans ended the decade by completing several hard-fought changes that had been coming throughout the period. Foremost among these was the state's

Wyoming was the first state to allow women to vote.

acceptance of the 19th Amendment on July 2, 1919, which gave women the right to vote. The action contributed to the national acceptance process which was completed by August of 1920. The way would soon open for women to hold public offices throughout the state.

Another event that was to have a lasting impact was the statewide reorganization of public schools. Beginning with the first high school in Buffalo Center in 1896, Iowans rapidly modernized the state's school systems. In 1913, they had legislated that tax money would be used to finance books. 1911 saw state aid to high schools to train vocational education and agriculture teachers. The key method used when several county schools got together to form a few, more centrally located schools was the idea of bussing

Horse-drawn school buses

students from home to school. By 1919, horse drawn school buses were an important part of every district school. Consolidation, or combining of schools, was not popular with many people, who thought larger schools would not be as good for students as smaller ones. Many people were also worried that they would not have as big a voice in how the school was run and what would be taught if they went with another school.

The bussing of school children only added to the demand for Iowa to improve the state's roads. By the end of the decade, there were over 171,000 cars on Iowa farms, not to mention trucks and tractors. With the number of vehicles increasing so rapidly, the state highway commission was formed in 1904, but got little help until the federal government made money available to pay for highway construction in 1916. The major push for hard surfaced roads was still yet to come. It would be another nine years until the election of Governor John Hammill, who became known as the "governor who pulled Iowa out of the mud."

The increase in bussing and motorized vehicles made it necessary to improve the state's roads.

All these improvements meant farmers would be able to transport their grain and livestock themselves, but the improvements also meant increased taxes. In Iowa, as in agricultural regions generally, farm land bore a large share of the burden of taxation. By 1920, even though prices were half what they had been in 1914, the taxes farmers paid were twice as high. The farmers objected because the taxes were figured on how much land ran near the new roads.

The strain felt by the farmers was starting to spread to the rest of the society, as shown by the 167 bank failures in 1920. Soon the rest of the country would feel the sting of the worst depression in our nation's history. The hard times of the past would be nothing when compared to the future. But the challenges would forge a new Iowa, better able to deal with the world. The salad days of farming were gone, as were big profits for most factories and other businesses. The state and the nation were sliding into a new period, where the rules of life would be changed.

CHAPTER XI

Iowans, in the years after 1920, would soon learn the lessons that we now know. This period, more than any other, saw the end of what was known as agri<u>culture</u> and the beginning of what we now call agri<u>business</u>. Whereas before 1920, life resembled in many ways the life after the Civil War; after 1920, life had more in common with today.

Life during this period had some things in common with other periods. The farmers' struggle against the elements, the need for transportation, and the trading of crops for money and other goods remained the same.

Iowa, in 1920, was a state still benefitting from the high prices of farm land and produce that set records during World War I. It was a state of highly inflated land prices, where land was often purchased with more hope than money. Many farmers had paid for less than 10% of the value of the farm they operated. Six and one-half million farms existed in 1920 in the U.S., and nothing was done to start a coordinated program of orderly slowing down from war time to peace time production. The federal government's support of market prices ended on March 21, 1920. The result was that millions of farmers tried but failed helplessly as the free market forced them to sell at lower and lower prices. The prices went down because of overproduction. The same amount or more was being produced for fewer people. The law of supply and demand affected this situation. If supplies are low

193

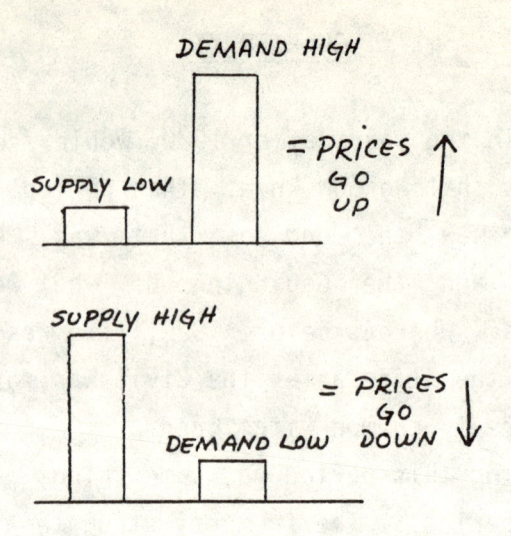

and demand for them is high, prices go up. If supply is high and demand low, prices go down.

Many farmers had been encouraged by high wartime prices and had mortgaged their farms to buy more land and machinery to expand their operations. When rural credit disappeared along with the government price supports, selling out was the only answer. Farm prices and land values fell, but taxes and interest rates remained high. Many farmers were soon in trouble. Towns and cities were affected as the farmers spent less money there. With so many Iowans in this position, land prices sank, and farmers were hard-pressed for buyers.

This period is a story of chain reactions that occur in a society when rapid change takes place. For example, in Iowa (like most rural states) after 1920, the low prices farmers received for their produce was a fact of life. Farmers were making less money, which meant many of them couldn't make the payments on their land and machinery at the local bank. In some cases, banks loaned farmers more money, and when the farmer couldn't make the payments, the bank had to close, taking the savings of all the people who put money in with it. Banks had no insured savings accounts then. During the 1920's, over 300 banks failed in Iowa.

If word got out that a bank might be in trouble, many people would rush to withdraw their savings. Much bank money is always out on loan and can't be recovered quickly. If too many people rushed to withdraw, the bank was forced to close.

In other cases, the bank took over the mortgage of the farm. This meant the bank would take over full ownership. The farmer lost his land, moved to town, or stayed on as a tenant farmer, one who rents the land, either for money or a share of the crop. Hence the term, sharecropper: a person who shares the crop

195

but isn't paid in cash was born. In either case, the community lost people, causing local businesses that depended on them to close down. With fewer people buying manufactured goods, factories laid off workers, which meant more unemployment in the cities.

Though this was a common state of affairs through the 20's in rural Iowa, it did not occur in many larger towns and cities. All through the 20's, rural poverty existed side by side with urban wealth. Our society changed as banks and insurance companies gained more and more land. There were fewer rural people in the middle class. There were over 2500 foreclosures in 1924 alone. Soon a large part of the state's farm land was controlled, not by farmers, but by bankers and insurance companies. This was land they had obtained for a fraction of the market value. By 1935, almost two (2) million acres that had belonged to Iowa farmers, now belonged to insurance companies. This meant that less money was in the hands of individuals. Instead of 2500 individual businesses putting money back into the farm, spending money in town and keeping the money local, much of it went to large cities or out of the state.

It was not until the stock market crash of August 1929, that the rest of the nation was plunged into a depression similar to the one the farmers had known for the past ten years. A depression is said to exist when people have no money to spend, which limits buying and selling, and the majority of the population is unemployed with no source of income. The depression

"Bread line" during the Great Depression of 1929.

that followed the stock market crash of 1929 is known as the Great Depression, and it affected not just Iowans and Americans, but everyone all over the world as well. So much of what modern Iowa and the U.S. is today, began in those bleak years of the 1930's. The fact that rural areas have electricity, that we have many national parks and recreation areas, or that people who retire have social security incomes is due to the reaction of Americans to the crisis that engulfed those years.

For many of us born in the last 25 years, it may seem hard to understand or even imagine the utter desperation of life for the majority of Iowans of those years. Such a combination of great problems had not happened before or since. The 30's were a time when people burned corn instead of coal, because corn

Edwin T. Meredith

was ten cents a bushel and coal was $3.00 a bushel. In 1929, 3,000,000 people were out of work in the United States. By 1930, 4,000,000 people were unemployed. On the farms, hogs had gone from 90 cents a pound to 3 cents a pound.

Strange as it may seem, the lack of government support for farmers came during the years when Iowa was home for a record number of people in authority in Washington. Following "Tama" Jim Wilson as Secretary of Agriculture in 1913, was Edwin T. Meredith of Des Moines, 1920, and later Henry C. Wallace, editor of the Wallace's Farmer, one of the pioneer agricultural newspapers of the state. Not only that, but Herbert Hoover, born in West Branch, was Secretary of Commerce.

While it is true that Hoover was elected President in 1928 as the first president born west of the Mississippi River, it should be pointed out that he

Herbert Hoover was born in West Branch, Iowa.

was not the choice for the nominee by the Republicans of Iowa. Hoover was a mining engineer representing California, who had long ago forgotten what farming was like. His record as Secretary of Commerce was one opposed to almost every farm bill proposed. It was no surprise, therefore, that Iowans opposed Hoover's nomination as a presidential nominee by an 81 percent margin.

Throughout the state there were great political changes. Radical groups appeared in some of the larger Iowa cities. Davenport had a socialist government and Sioux City had a labor government. Since 1857, all the governors of Iowa, except one, had been Republicans. Most of the representatives and all of the senators from Iowa to Washington had been Republicans. But in 1924, Iowa sent its first Democratic senator, Daniel Steck, to Washington. From 1932 to 1938, all the governors were Democrats.

Another reaction to this terrible situation was the beginning of a new farm movement. These farmers, tired of looking to Washington or Des Moines for help, turned to one of their own organizations, the Farmers Union, for action and ideas. Though the Farmers Union had its origins in the South in 1902, it had gradually spread north and west until, by 1929, most of the members lived in the midwest. Although Iowans had not organized a farm union group until 1917, during the depressed 20's the growth of the Farmer's Union was impressive. By 1927, the Iowa Farmer's Union had found a dynamic and impulsive president, Milo Reno, whose farm program was simply stated: cost of production plus a reasonable profit for the farmer. This is often referred to as parity. Now with farm prices far below the cost of production, farmers were ready to listen, even to revolt.

The first acts of violence occurred in the summer and fall of 1931, when farmers of Cedar and Muscatine counties and other areas took direct action to prevent further testing of their cattle for bovine tuberculosis in what came to be known as "the Cow War". Even though such testing had been going on in Iowa since 1919 on a voluntary basis, in 1929 it became compulsory, meaning it must be done. Iowa farmers have never been much for being told what to do, especially when the veterinarians were from out of town. These "outsiders" would move into a county, test the cattle, remove those cows who reacted to the test, and destroy them. The farmer was then paid back

The Farmer's Union.

by the state for the infected cow's value. By 1931, many farmers were saying that the cows were worth more than the state was paying. There was also a rumor going around, though it was not true, that the test was inaccurate. All this came to a head during the summer of 1931, when there happened to be a high incidence of tuberculosis in the area around Tipton and Muscatine. When one farmer after another began to lose an entire herd, the farmers armed themselves and blocked the entry of state veterinaries to their farm.

In response, recently elected Governor Dan Turner, from Corning, declared martial law, and sent 2500 National Guard troops to Tipton and other areas to enforce the law. The testing continued under armed guard.

The Cow War was the beginning of the Farmer's Holiday movement that was bent on keeping produce and livestock from the market in order to force prices up

Farmer's Holiday movement

to an acceptable level. The thinking was: if there is less supply and more or the same demand, prices will go up.

Unlawful "prairie law" was applied particularly to prevent or to interrupt mortgage sales. "Prairie Law" was based on the idea that it was not right that all a man's possessions could be sold against his will even though it was lawful. It was a system whereby large numbers of unhappy farmers would show up at a sale to harass or bother the people who were trying to sell the farm. It took a very brave outsider surrounded by great numbers of hostile people to bid against them. Many times if buyers knew there was to be a demonstration at an auction, they would not show up. Then the farmer's friends would bid very low prices and return the farm and its machinery to the original owner.

Farmer's Holiday road block

In April, the height of such violent opposition to disagreeable legal processes was reached when a LeMars judge was mobbed for refusing to sign papers that would have stopped foreclosures. This representative of the law was beaten, forcibly taken from the Court House, and threatened with lynching.

At this same time in 1932, a similar "Farmer's Holiday" movement occurred around Sioux City. Most farmers refused to bring crops or livestock to market in an effort to bring the supply down. They blockaded roads and refused to let any produce come through. There were many instances of violence as some trucks tried to go through loaded with farm produce. Farmer pickets stood against truckers. When a trucker was shot and died the next day, the sheriff of Plymouth county called the governor for help. He declared martial law and called out the National Guard to again restore order. More than 100 were arrested, and makeshift jails of barbed wire were set up.

Dry summers and hard winters were experienced during the 1930's.

Thus twice within 18 months, armed might of the state was used against its own citizens--conservative Republican farmers who were now in revolt against the government.

Nature too seemed stacked against Iowans as drought dried up and blew away precious top soil and crops during the driest years on record of 1930, 1934, and 1936. The 1930's marked an end to the old practices, both industrial and rural. All unemployed parts of society called for help from Washington. However, President Hoover believed that the government should interfere as little as possible with people's lives. He felt the individuals should try to work out their own problems. As a result, Hoover's name was linked with everything that was wrong with the country. Groups of paper shacks where homeless unemployed lived were called "Hoovervilles", and newspapers used as covers or insulation were "Hoover blankets". Many people who were formerly making good wages were forced

"Hoovervilles" were shacks where homeless unemployed lived during the 1930's.

to sell apples on street corners or to leave their families to try and find work. Because of this, many people lost their self-respect and felt worthless. Many men deserted their families and wandered the countryside.

Franklin Delano Roosevelt promised that if he were elected president, he would do something about the terrible conditions and restore the nation's self-respect. Iowa and the United States believed him, and he was elected by a landslide of votes in 1932. Iowans were told they could now expect a "New Deal".

Shortly after his election, Roosevelt appointed Henry A. Wallace, an Iowan who had long been the Editor of the Wallace's Farmer, to serve as Secretary of Agriculture, a post Wallace's father had held in the early 1920's. Wallace masterminded many of the

205

"New Deal" programs that benefitted farmers. Before Henry Wallace retired, he would become Vice President under Franklin D. Roosevelt in 1940, Secretary of Commerce under Harry S. Truman's administration and presidential candidate in 1948.

Henry A. Wallace
1888-1965

The next eight years saw the development of a number of federal programs that benefitted and maybe saved many Iowans. The miners around Granger were one group that suffered through the hard times, but improved themselves through a federal program. They were only working a few hours each week and they were living in shacks with no electricity, insulation, heat, running water or toilet facilities. When government funds were made available, the miners built 50 modern homes themselves, raised their own vegetables and became able to take good care of themselves.

The changes occuring during this time compounded the problems of other miners. The increased use of natural gas diminished the demand for Iowa coal. The late 1920's and 30's spelled the end of many coal mines, and coal mining towns disappeared across Iowa. These groups of workers headed for the cities, adding to the bread lines of the urban unemployed.

A far-reaching depression program was the "corn loan" which guaranteed farmers a minimal price for their corn and allowed them to borrow 45 cents a bushel for any corn they stored and didn't sell. In order to keep supply down, the government later paid the farmers to destroy their stored surplus. The Agriculture Adjustment Act guaranteed prices if farmers would not raise crops on land they had formerly used. These programs didn't solve all the farm problems, but they kept thousands of farms from total disaster.

Another depression program, the Civilian Conservation Corps was organized in 1933 to provide jobs for unemployed young men and veterans. Men enrolled in the CCC camps, as they were known, and got paid about $6 per week, half of which had to be sent home. If this doesn't sound like much, remember, a month's electricity bill was $1. The CCC men also were given housing, medical care, food and clothing. The camps reminded one of an army camp populated by civilians. The people who signed up worked on soil conservation, flood control and forestry projects. Many of Iowa's state parks were improved through the work of these men from the CCC camps. The program continued until 1941.

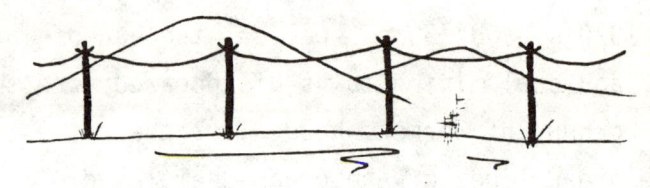

Cooperative associations built highlines to provide electricity for farms.

Perhaps one of the most lasting of Roosevelt's New Deal programs which would make a profound change for Iowans was The Rural Electrification Administration started in 1935. It authorized United States government loans to bring electricity to farms. Up until then, only one in ten farms had electricity. Electric companies didn't believe farmers needed electricity. "Besides," they argued, "it is too expensive to put up the poles and wires."

An early radio

All across Iowa, communities organized cooperative associations to build electrical lines to farms to provide electricity for farmers' use. By 1940, over 66,000 of Iowa farms had electricity. Soon farm families were enjoying the benefits of electric refrigerators, radios, fans, running water, and indoor plumbing.

The largest government program that benefited Iowa then and since was the WPA - the Works Progress Administration. It employed 37,000 Iowans. These workers built public buildings, schools, Iowa's extensive farm to market roads, bridges and sewer lines. In many cases, because of their excellent construction, the buildings and lines are still being used. With hard surfaced farm to market roads, the farm family was no longer cut off from everyone. Gradually, the way of life on the farm became more like that of the city.

The New Deal program that has affected the most people since then is the Social Security program. This was designed to help elderly people whose savings had been wiped out. It was meant to help supplement the small savings people had. It was one of the few New Deal programs to continue after World War I.

As Europe slipped steadily toward war in 1938 and 1939, Europeans began stock-piling food and manufactured goods for the years ahead. It is no coincidence that 1938 is usually given as the year the Great Depression ended.

By 1940, the U.S. was supplying the allied countries of Europe with a wide variety of arms and supplies. All this meant jobs for Americans and a return to prosperity.

In Iowa, farm prices began to rise and industries formerly engaged in making farm machinery began to manufacture military equipment.

When Japan attacked Pearl Harbor on December 7, 1941, the U.S. entered the war, with an economy that was already well on the way to meeting the needs of the American war effort.

Iowans registered in large numbers for the military draft with 262,638 men and women entering military service. By the end of the war, 8,398 had died to preserve the American way of life.

It is strange that a discovery made in the depths of the depression was to lift farming and Iowa into a modern age, a development with so much impact that agriculture prior to World War I would look very old fashioned by comparison. It was an factor perfected in Iowa, by Iowans, but would soon be responsible for feeding the masses of the world. That development was hybrid seed corn. The term hybrid refers to the process of the controlled crossing of different types of the same plant, so that the best traits of each are joined into one. Not only does this result in higher yields, but hybrid plants are more uniform in height and more resistant to weather and insects. Before, these plants were grown from seeds taken from the last harvest. Using hybrids, the strongest and best plants could be used to raise even stronger and better plants.

Few major developments in creating hybrid seed had occurred before 1917, when the first successful single cross between two different types of corn was made by Donald Jones of Illinois. By 1922, the Iowa State University Experimental Station began the task of

% OF FARMS USING HYBRID SEED

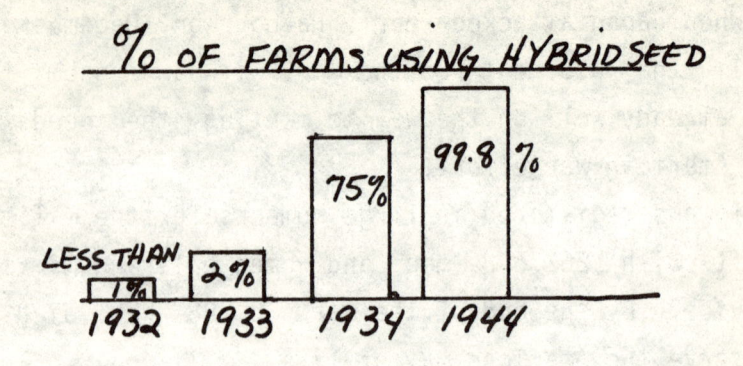

1932	1933	1934	1944
LESS THAN 1%	2%	75%	99.8%

perfecting the best combination of plant characteristics, performing the many thousands of tests which would provide the answer. By 1932, Iowa State College put the first hybrid seed corn on the market. In the spring of the following year, a few farmers, at the bottom of the depression, who were adventurous enough to try anything to increase their income, and with enough money in hand to buy the seed, planted their field with hybrid seed corn. Not many could afford it, less than one percent in fact. With the following harvest however, word spread and the next spring almost two percent of the fields were planted with hybrid seed. By 1939, 3/4 of all corn acreage was involved, and by 1944, 99.8 percent was planted with hybrid seed. With better corn crops, Iowa's average yields doubled--from 21.9 bushels per acre in 1934 to 41.9 in 1944.

Another development with equal impact was the introduction to Iowa farmers of the soybean from the Orient. The Iowa State University Experimental Station began work on the soybean as early as 1910, by testing over 3,000 varieties and strains brought in from China. At first, used largely as a forage crop, the soybean came into its own during World War II as a source of oil and high protein food. Today the soybean is one of Iowa's major crops.

After 1946, trends that had begun in Iowa before, but were slowed by the lack of money in the depression years, now accelerated.

Primary among these changes was the migration of a sizeable share of Iowa's population from farms to cities. Leland Sage, an Iowa historian, points out four major reasons for this:

1) increased machinery on farms, less need for manpower
2) increased urban industry (need for labor)
3) cheap land was a thing of the past
4) decline of European immigration, a group that had often taken up the slack in farm population in the past when others had moved on.

Industrial centers grew rapidly, causing cities near them to grow as well. In Iowa, by the end of 1947, twice as many people were working in manufacturing as in 1939. In those same years the value of Iowa's manufactured products tripled.

As we have seen, Iowa has had a meaningful history and has been an important force in the nation. Its economic impact on the nation has been a very significant factor. Its agricultural productivity has become an important issue throughout the world. It will play a bigger role as food becomes more of an issue in the future.

Now that we know of Iowa's rich history, it remains for you, as a student, to find out how your town, family and you fit into that history and what role you will play in the future.

This is the challenge.

Agriculture, 141-146, 152-155,
  158-161, 166-168, 170, 176-182,
  185, 193, 200-204
Allisen, William, 175
Archaic Indians, 23-24
Belknap, W. W., 134
Beltrami, G. C., 70
Bering Strait, 19
Black Hawk, 72-77
Black Hawk War, 72-75
Blacks, 128-130, 138
Bluegrass Palace, 164
Boies, Horace, 172-173
Boundaries, 105-108
Brown, John, 130-132
Burlington, 98
Butter, 151
Capitol (Des Moines), 119-122
Catten, George, 70
Civil War, 132-136
Civilian Conservation Corps, 208
Claims Clubs, 81
Clarke, William, 131
Coal, 7-8
Coal Palace, 164
Conservation, 155
Constitution, 104-106, 110
Copperheads, 136
Coppoc, Edwin and Barclay, 131-132
Corn Palace, 164
Cow War, 200-204
Cream separator, 150-151
Creamery, 150-151
Crop Rotation, 152-154
Cummins, Albert, 175
Delisle, William, 43
DeNoyelles, Major, 44
Depression, 169-170, 189, 192,
  194-195, 204-205
Des Moines, 119-120
Dodge, B. M., 134, 137
Dragoons, 87, 104
Drake, Frances, 174
Drought, 170, 204
Dubuque, Julian, 49-50
Economics, 166-167, 193-194
Effigy Mounds, 28
English, 39
Farmer's Union, 200
Farmers Holiday, 201, 203-204
Feedlots, 153
Fort Madison, 61-63
French, 39, 45, 52-53
Ft. Armstrong, 65

Ft. Atkinson, 69
Fur Trade, 43, 45-47
Giard, Basil, 51
Glaciers, 10-17
Glenwood Culture, 31
Grange, 158
Grasshoppers, 143-144
Great Oasis Culture, 29-30
Greenback Party, 143, 174
Grinnell, Josiah, 116, 131
Halfbreed Tract, 67-68
Hammill, John, 191
Harlan, James, 137
Hogs, 153
Honey War, 97-98
Hoover, Herbert, 198-199
Hopewell Indians, 25-28
Hybred Corn, 211-212
Ice Age, 2, 10-17
Igneous Rock, 1-3
Illinoian Glacier, 14
Immigrants, 82-83, 116-117,
  147-150
Indians
  General, 34-37, 56-58
  Hopewell, 25-28
  Ioway, 33-34
  Mesquakie, 34-37, 44, 104, 118
  Oneota, 32-33
  Paleo, 20-24
  Sauk, 34-37, 44, 72-75, 92, 104
  Sioux, 34-37, 111
  Winnebago, 68-69
  Woodland, 24-37
Iowa City, 99, 119
Iowa Territory, 95
Ioway Indians, 33-34
Jackson, Frank, 171
Jefferson, Thomas, 52-55, 58
Joliet, Louis, 39-42
Kansan Glacier, 14
Kearny, Stephen, 66-67, 87-88
Kelly's Army, 171
Kirkwood, Samuel, 133
Lewis and Clark Expedition, 53-56
Lincoln, Abraham, 73, 132-133
Livestock, Purebred, 160-161
Loess, 15
Long, Major, 65
Louisiana Territory, 52-55
Lucas, Robert, 96-97
Mail, 168
Marin, Pierre Paul, 43
Marquette, Fr. Jacques, 39-42

Marryat, Fredrick, 70
Meredith, Edwin, 198
Mesquakie Indians, 34-37, 44, 92, 104, 118
Michigan Territory, 89
Mill Creek Culture, 30-31
Mormons, 112-114, 117-118
Murray, Charles, 70
Nebraskan Glacier, 14
Neutral Zone, 68-69
New Deal, 205, 207-210
Newspaper, Agricultural, 160
Nichollett, Joseph, 69
Oats, 154
Old Zion, 91
Oneota Indians, 32
Packing House, 153, 155
Paleo Indians, 20-23
Perrot, Nicholas, 42
Pike, Zebulon, 58-60
Populist Party, 174-175
Primary, 176
Prohibition, 162
Railroads, 122-126, 139, 152, 155-157
Reno, Milo, 200
Republican Party, 127, 173-174
Roads, 191, 209
Rocks, 1-11
Roosevelt, Franklin, 205
Rural Electrification Administration, 208
Sauk Indians, 34-37, 44, 72-75, 92, 104
Saukenuk, 71
Schoolcraft, Henry, 69
Schools, 190-191
Scott, Winfield, 75
Seas, 4-9
Sedimentary Rock, 2,4
Settlers, 79-81, 83-86, 99-100
Sioux Indians, 34-37, 111
Soybean, 212
Spanish, 39, 49-51
Spanish-American War, 172
Speculator, 99, 137
Squatters, 78-79
Steamboats, 86
Swamps, 7
Tabor, 116
Taylor, Zachery, 63
Telephones, 168
Tesson, Louis Honore, 51-52
Todd, John, 116

Tractor, 180
Transportation, 130-133
Treaty of 1804, 56-58
Turner, Dan, 201
Underground Railroad, 128-129
Wallace, Henry A., 205-206
Wallace, Henry C., 198
War of 1812, 62-64
Weaver, Baird, 175
Wheat, 145-146
Wilson, Jim, 198
Winnebago Indians, 68
Wisconsin Glacier, 14
Wisconsin Territory, 89-91, 95
Women's Sufferage, 176, 190
Woodland Indians, 24-37
Works Progress Administration, 209
World War I, 182-187
World War II, 210-211

Bertha Bartlett Public Library
503 Broad Street
Story City, IA 50248